T0313449

Desert Ascetics
of Egypt

PAST IMPERFECT

See further
www.arc-humanities.org/our-series/pi

Desert Ascetics of Egypt

Darlene L. Brooks Hedstrom

British Library Cataloguing in Publication Data
A catalogue record for this book is available from the British Library

ISBN (print) 9781641891677
e-ISBN (PDF) 9781802700817
e-ISBN (EPUB) 9781802700824

www.arc-humanities.org
Printed and bound in the UK (by CPI Group [UK] Ltd), USA (by Bookmasters), and elsewhere using print-on-demand technology.

Contents

List of Illustrations

Introduction

Travelling into the Desert

Paphnutius was tired and hungry. As a monk, he was accustomed to limited sleep and food, but on this day, he found himself truly exhausted and in need of rest. After many days of travelling by foot through the remotest parts of Egypt's deserts, he found the perfect place to recover. He was drawn to the location by the fragrance of fruit trees that reminded him of the gardens he once played in as a boy. He prayed momentarily as he considered the promise of the sweetness of Paradise and hoped that he would soon find the source of the pleasing aroma.

When he returned his gaze to the horizon, he saw the trees clustered together around a mud brick and daub well. He saw the leaves of the date palms swaying gently as they held onto clusters of dates. He could also identify trees bearing citrons, pomegranates, figs, and nectarines. Other trees, whose names Paphnutius had now long forgotten, sat nestled between them, along with grapevines. Sheltered from the sun and the desert heat, the monk sat down and fell into a deep and restful sleep as he was comforted by the shade. He dreamed of the planted trees in the desert.

Paphnutius awoke refreshed. He was slightly surprised when he looked to the horizon and saw four figures emerging as if from nowhere. He knew that the oasis he had found was likely a common gathering place along the desert road for other travellers. As the figures came closer, Paphnutius could see that they radiated beauty, much like the trees surrounding him. They wore sheepskin garments made of the finest skins, very different from the rougher quality skins that he and his fellow monks usually wore. He looked down briefly to see his own garment, slightly torn, bearing marks of his work as a bookbinder, and dirt from his weeks of travel. He looked up again to see the men now in front of him.

He was overjoyed to see them. They were exactly the type of holy individuals he was hoping to meet when he began his journey into the deepest deserts. He thought they were angelic beings; as they came closer, his whole body was filled with joy and a profound sense of calm. The four strangers spoke, "Greetings, Paphnutius, our beloved brother."[1] He immediately fell to the ground to kiss their feet as a sign of his profound gratitude. He was overwhelmed to hear his own name uttered by the beautiful strangers. They then pulled him to his feet and began feeding him fruit from the nearby trees. Paphnutius felt as if he was in Paradise.

After a week of being fed by the men, Paphnutius felt brave enough to ask the men where they grew up and where they were travelling from when he met them. The question of identity was an important one because Paphnutius knew, as did most monks, that strangers could mask their real identities and pose as either demons seeking to derail one's asceticism or as angels offering encouragement and nourishment. The men presented themselves as angelic beings, and Paphnutius needed to know the truth.

The four men responded by stating that it was God himself who urged them to find Paphnutius to teach him about their ascetic way of life. Paphnutius felt humbled that God would reward his pursuit of deeper asceticism with this meeting at the tree grove oasis. The men identified themselves as residents originally from Pemje, the Coptic name for a town in central Egypt that was known in Greek as Oxyrhynchus. The men, who were at least in their seventies, told Paphnutius that they

---

1 Paphnutius, *Life of Onnophrius*, in *Histories of the Monks of Upper Egypt and the Life of Onnophrius*, trans. Tim Vivian (Kalamazoo: Cistercian, 1993), 162.

had been friends since childhood. Their fathers were powerful officials in the city and sent their sons to school together. Eager to learn, the four boys applied themselves to their studies, mastering both Coptic and Greek. But, after several years, they found themselves desiring more than the wisdom of the world; now, they wanted to learn the wisdom of God.

The determined friends set out from Pemje with a week's worth of dried bread to sustain them on their journey out to the western desert. After several days, they found themselves in the heart of the desert. They stopped when they met a person whose whole body radiated light; this was clearly an angel of God. The stranger guided the four men to the tree grove oasis, where they met an old monk who could teach the young men the wisdom of God. For the next year, they studied with him until his death. Then the four friends spent the next sixty years living in the desert, alone, gathering once a week at the grove to receive holy communion. Paphnutius was in awe of the aged men, whose way of life was clearly like that of the angels.

At the conclusion of their tale, Paphnutius was overwhelmed by the smell of a new fragrance. He knew it was the scent of holiness, and he almost instinctively rose to his feet. The angel of God stood before the men, fed them communion, and departed. Paphnutius had never experienced an encounter with an angel and, overwhelmed by the holiness of the moment, collapsed to the ground. His companions revived him, and they all spent the night praying.

Paphnutius offered a word of thanks to his fellow ascetics and then saw the angel of God before him. The angel instructed him to return to Egypt, meaning the outer desert with its nearby shale and limestone cliffs and the Nile valley with its agricultural fields. Once there, Paphnutius was directed to share the story of his encounter with the four men and their sixty-year residence in the desert. Through Paphnutius's storytelling, more monks would be inspired to seek out the monastic life as the men of Pemje had before him. Paphnutius and the four men walked together for six miles before Paphnutius turned and asked them for their names. They revealed their names as

John, Andrew, Heraklamon, and Theophilus; and they begged Paphnutius to share their names and story with those he would meet. Although Paphnutius did not know where he was at the time, it was later revealed to him that the four monks were living in the desert of Sketis, one of the most important centres for desert asceticism in Egypt.

The story of Paphnutius and the four monks of the fruit grove is one of thousands that exist from the fifth century, when Christians composed stories of famous ascetics living in the Egyptian deserts. The story contains important elements of the monastic movement, such as the importance of communion, encounters with divine and human beings, and the value of spiritual instruction in the ways of asceticism. What is missing from the story, however, is the material world that defined the lives of the five monks.

Desert Ascetics of Egypt

Other monastic stories tell us about the daily challenges and miracles of living in the desert. Sometimes the stories are deceptively short, and yet they offer insight into the interior life of monks. These stories served as didactic tools for future generations as to how one might cultivate a holy life, respond to temptations, and foster a close relationship with God. The stories evolved as training manuals for others who wanted guidance in how to live a holy life. It was necessary to make a daily martyrdom of the self, whose various temptations inhibited a monk's progress in being fully mindful of the divine. In the story of Paphnutius we do not hear of the interior life of the monks, but only of the miraculous fact of their solitary life, entirely dependent upon God.

In contrast, the stories of Amma Sarah of Pelusia are more typical of the accounts of Desert Ascetics than the encounters of Paphnutius, in that the stories comprise short accounts, sometimes only a few lines, in which the wise words of a monk provided the miraculous elements of how an ascetic lived in the desert. Amma Sarah was well known and respected by male monks, who went to visit her for spiritual benefit. She had lived sixty years in Pelusia, and was known for her determination to please God. She did not seek out the praise of fellow monks, for she knew that many would not approve of a woman living the monastic life. In one account, two male monks travelled to visit her to undermine her commitment; they also tried to shame her because of her gender. In response, Sarah told the old men that she was a man in her thoughts and that her female-gendered body was irrelevant to her asceticism. Recognizing the power dynamics of the visit with the monks, she concluded by stating that the men were women because of their thoughts.

In another story of Amma Sarah, we learn she struggled with *porneia*, a Greek word that means uncontrollable sexual desire. *Porneia* was a frequent sin experienced in the body and often discussed by male monks, who struggled with the desire for real and imagined women. The recognition of female desire in Sarah's life demonstrates that all male and female monks faced challenges in addressing sexual needs. Sarah addressed her temptation by asking God not to remove it; instead, she used the desire as an opportunity to battle bodily temptation with God's help. Her persistence was praised, as she spent thirteen of her sixty years working to control this desire.

Sarah's stories reveal the importance of emulation for a successful monastic life. Just as she became a spiritual mother to monks who visited her, Paphnutius also became a spiritual father, by teaching others about the monks whom he encountered on his journey into the desert. Both monks recounted stories of themselves and others. The stories offered evidence of God's miraculous support of desert asceticism. But the stories are incomplete, because they skim over the actual lived experience of desert life.

Sources for Studying the Desert Ascetics of Egypt

The exact origins of many monastic stories, such as the ones above, are not entirely clear. However, by the fifth and sixth centuries, monastic editors had collected and published a series of stories known as the *Sayings of the Desert Fathers* and Mothers. The most popular editions are three Greek collections. The *Alphabetical* collection organizes the stories according to the names of one hundred and seventeen monks, following the Greek alphabet. The *Anonymous* collection is a much larger corpus of sayings, but they are perhaps less known because they are not always linked to famous individuals, thereby diminishing the popularity and mythologizing nature of the stories. The anonymity of the individuals within each account also inhibits our ability to place the stories in time and space, further removing the stories from a grounding in a physical landscape of memory about the Egyptian deserts. The *Systematic* collection is the result of monastic editors attempting to cluster stories around monastic themes rather than named individuals. The selected stories showcase some of the *Alphabetic* and *Anonymous* sayings to offer a training manual for monks facing a variety of issues.

The *Alphabetic, Anonymous*, and *Systematic Sayings of the Desert Fathers and Mothers* are interconnected traditions that build a story of the great Desert Ascetics of Egypt.[2] The translation of the stories into Latin, where the stories were known either as *Apophthegmata Patrum* or as *Verba Seniorum*, ensured the popularity of the texts, along with later copies translated into Coptic, Syriac, Ge'ez, Armenian, Arabic, and Slavonic languages. The transmission history of the sayings reveals the appeal of the first ascetics as guides for how to live, but also reveals the allure of a time when miracles and healings were thought to be more common. The sayings are presented as the actual words of the first monks of the desert. But how reliable are these statements? And is reliabil-

---

2 The relationship between the three main collections is explained in the Further Reading below. Reference to the *Alphabetic Sayings* is noted by the named monastic mother or father followed by the "Sayings" number for that monk, such as Antony 5, Sarah 8, or Theodore of Pherme 1. References are to *Give Me a Word*, trans. Wortley. References to the *Systematic Sayings* are noted as *AP.S.* followed by the book and section number: see *The Books of Elders*, trans. Wortley.

ity necessary? For historians, the challenge is to sift through the various accounts, build a profile of what other Christians saw and experienced when visiting monastic communities, and use archaeological evidence to fill in the gaps whenever possible. The spartan nature of the monastic sayings reflects a complex oral tradition and history.

In approaching the *Sayings* it is important to note that their genre offers little in terms of historical events which might be traced back to the actual monks referenced in the texts. The stories also lack substantive engagement with political events or even with key theological issues, adopting instead a generic tone without direct commentary on any particular moment in time. Given that the church underwent a variety of theological disputes at this time, it is perhaps not surprising that the sayings are more neutral in tone and do not engage with many theological debates. For example, in the *Sayings* there are few indications of the ongoing controversy about the nature of Jesus and the divisions that separated the Coptic and Syrian Christians from other Christians in Jerusalem, Constantinople, and Rome. Instead, the *Sayings* offer directions on how to approach God, how to face one's own demons, and how to treat others. Rather than a mirror to a moment in time, the *Sayings* are a mirror to what it means to be human: living with oneself and living with others.

The *Sayings* are not our only sources for studying desert asceticism. Scholars of monasticism now consider a wide array of sources from the fourth and fifth century: hagiographies, travelogues, personal letters, graffiti, tax accounts, wills, and ecclesiastical histories. All are read alongside the accounts of the Desert Ascetics. Additionally, an increased interest in monasticism and early Christian communities has spawned new excavation projects which offer different materials for considering early monasticism as it is represented in sites, burials, buildings, and portable objects. Excavations also provide new papyrological evidence that illustrates how monks interacted with each other and the nonmonastic community around them.

Each body of evidence reflects the motives of its writers or makers, and in turn reveals the concerns of the community for whom the texts were written or the materials were made. Sometimes, written sources are divided into two, broad categories: literary and documentary sources. Literary sources include texts for whom a wide audience or readership is expected. The *Life of Antony*, written by Bishop Athanasius, and the *Sayings of the Desert Fathers and Mothers* were intended to be instructive for many readers and listeners. The author and editors were attuned to the potential longevity their works might have for the new Christian communities. The literary texts, sometimes referred to as *high texts*, may serve as religious inspiration, in the case of Christian audiences, or as didactic tools for other monks seeking models for how to live. Travelogues, like the lives of saints, are highly structured texts intended for broad readership, serving as inspirational literature for Christian readers who could not travel. They are miniature hagiographies but also expanded sayings, which present stories intended to guide and instruct. While the historical elements of particular individuals may be harder to highlight in these works, we can see how Christian authors constructed the lives of saints and what meaning the literature had for monastic and lay readers.

In contrast, documentary sources such as tax records, letters written to a monk, or bills of sale were written for a particular person or community; readership in this case is small and associated with a particular event. Unlike ecclesiastical histories or hagiographies, which were copied and reproduced for dissemination, documentary sources have a more limited lifespan in terms of readership and community memory. The Coptic and Greek documentary evidence from Egypt offers insights into religious changes that might not be readily apparent in literary sources. For example, we may observe monks as spiritual intercessors: managing property, fetching food for someone's donkeys, or being patrons, all while being identified by one of several terms. Letters reveal how desert ascetics were identified and described by others. One person may be called a *monachos*, someone who lived alone, while another may be an *apotaktikos*, someone who renounced what they owned. Still another may be called *anachōrētēs*, someone who retreated from the world. In many cases, even a single letter might include two or more of these terms for the same person, revealing the fluidity of language used to describe the monastic movement in its earliest centuries.

For example, the name Paphnutius was a popular one in ancient Christian Egypt. Eight letters survive, on papyrus, from the mid-fourth century. These letters, from both women and men, were addressed to a monk named Paphnutius; he is not, however, the monk from the story above. This Paphnutius was well-connected to the world beyond his monastic dwelling. The letters capture the complex social networks of which Paphnutius was a part. His correspondents included civic elites, who were literate themselves, as well as those who had to hire a scribe for their correspondence. All wanted him to intercede on their behalf in some way. The letters sought his miraculous prayers to heal illness, his skills to resolve civic disputes, and his wisdom to restore one's confidence in God's power. The letters, unlike the story of the desert Paphnutius or Sarah's wise words, are examples of documentary evidence—a body of evidence that reflects a particular moment in time, written with a singular purpose, and often for a limited readership. The letters were not intended for spiritual edification for future communities, unlike the stories of Amma Sarah and Abba Paphnutius. Yet, if we read these letters to a monk in conjunction with popular monastic literature, we can build a more nuanced and comprehensive history of Desert Ascetics.

Some scholars elevate the value of documentary evidence over literary sources because the documents impart a greater sense of the *realia* of the time. These scholars argue that there is more intimacy with the past in documentary evidence than in the literary sources, which reflect the voices of powerful, elite authorities within the Christian monastic world. Yet, it would be a mistake to separate the two. When read together, both collections can add to our understanding of the Desert Ascetics and the history of desert monasticism.

Literary sources reveal important narratives of the past and the present. They demonstrate efforts to construct social and religious memory in ways that documentary sources cannot. Documentary evidence uncovers individuals, moments in times, and snippets of life that are never seen in the literary sources. When the sources are read together, they amplify and enrich our understanding of the past.

A final source of material for investigation into desert monasticism is the much broader category of archaeological evidence. This vast body of material includes documentary sources, which may be excavated from monastic sites, but also monastic buildings, footpaths between monasteries and nearby villages, viewsheds from the Nile to a monastery, wall paintings from a monk's house, a wooden stylus for writing, and broken vessels that once held a monk's daily meal. Such objects offer a different perspective on the physicality of the spiritual life of desert ascetics.[3] While many scholars know of the *Sayings*, few know about the wealth of archaeological material associated with monastic life and about how much material is preserved in Egypt, both in the Nile Valley and in the deserts. Much of this material directly reflects the world of the fifth century and later on, making the material remains a powerful context for examining the successors to the early Desert Ascetics. The material remains of early Christian communities, nonmonastic and monastic, do not appear until the late fourth century, when Christians started to produce objects and things that we may clearly associate with Christian iconography and culture. As archaeological work continues in Egypt, it is possible that more material may be recovered that dates back to the fourth century or earlier.

---

3 For a catalogue of objects found within written sources see Ludovic Bender et al., "Artefacts and Raw Materials in Byzantine Archival Documents / Objets et matériaux dans les documents d'archives byzantins," at http://typika.cfeb.org.

Overview of the Chapters

This book is a journey into the history of the Desert Ascetics of Egypt who lived during the third and fourth centuries and whose stories were told in the fifth and sixth centuries. These ascetics took up residency in a landscape that was filled with demons, both real and imagined, and established their lives around the daily work of prayer, instruction, and healing. They quickly became the subjects of various forms of religious travel, as Christians desired to witness their lives and miracles. The sources about the Desert Ascetics are diverse and include travelogues detailing encounters with ascetics, histories of early Christian communities, biographies of famous monks, and—lesser known but still important—archaeological evidence recovered from late antique Egypt.

By reading the literary and archaeological evidence together, we will explore how monks created a new, utopian lifestyle dedicated to God, outside of the physical and social structures of their time. Some monks moved to the edges of their society, such as the borders of their towns, farmsteads, fields, and districts, living together in the near desert but still visible from their prior towns and agricultural fields. Others chose to live in settlements near each other to create new communities of like-minded Christians. Still others went further away, avoiding community, noise, and societal obligations entirely, believing the words of an anonymous monk: "Do not hasten towards the city, but rather make haste to flee the city and you will be saved" (*AP.N.*130).[4]

The discussion here is not intended to be comprehensive of all the monks who would identify as desert dwellers. My focus in this book is on the Desert Ascetics of Egypt: on the sources that tell the stories of early monasticism; on what we can learn about the material culture of the earliest desert monks; and on how reading archaeology and textual sources

---

4 N.130 is one of the many *Anonymous Sayings of the Desert Fathers* (*AnonAP*). I use the numbering provided by *The Anonymous Sayings of the Desert Fathers*, trans. Wortley.

together provides a richer account of the monastic movement. Because I focus on the Desert Ascetics, the book does not explore the well-known coenobitic, or communal, forms of Egyptian monasticism in places such as southern Egypt, where Pachomius established monasteries in villages along the Nile and where Shenoute established three communities on the border of the agricultural fields and desert cliffs by Atripe.[5] Whereas Pachomius was well known outside of Egypt, Shenoute was not. Remarkably we have more pages of Shenoute's writings than any other figure from Late Antiquity. Further, the majority of the documentary sources reflect the world of male monks. Thus, for this short book, I focus primarily on male-gendered material.[6] The purpose of this book is to present a close study of the famous Egyptian Desert Ascetics in northwest Egypt and to consider the historicity of their stories, to examine the physical evidence of desert monasticism, and to better understand *how* the story of the Desert Ascetics of Egypt became larger than life in the history of monasticism.

Chapter One introduces the Desert Ascetics as early Christian celebrities who worked miracles, and places them into the historical and religious landscape of Egypt during the third and fourth centuries. I explain how monasticism was part of a growing interest in celibacy and virginity as an alternative to marriage. The chapter concludes with a broad context for the popular monastic literature that served for centuries as the definitive account of desert asceticism.

Chapter Two examines the most famous collection of monastic stories, the *Sayings of the Desert Fathers and Mothers*, as a source for how Desert Ascetics lived and what they taught. The stories were written nearly two hundred years

---

5 *Pachomian Koinonia*, trans. Armand Veilleux, 3 vols. (Kalamazoo: Cistercian, 1982). *The Canons of Our Fathers: Monastic Rules of Shenoute*, trans. Bentley Layton (Oxford: Oxford University Press, 2014).

6 Caroline T. Schroeder, "Women in Anchoritic and Semi-Anchoritic Monasticism in Egypt: Rethinking the Landscape," *Church History* 83, no. 1 (2014): 1–17.

after the lives of the first Desert Ascetics and are not, there-fore, eye-witness accounts of monasticism. Fortunately, we have some near-contemporary travelogues and biographies, known as hagiographies, which offer insight into how Christian communities understood the importance of monastic life. We will learn about the importance of monastic wonder-working and the miraculous healings that drew hundreds of Christians to visit the Desert Ascetics. I also survey some of the Ascetics' teachings, which ranged from deep theological reflections to snappy rebukes to compassionate insights on how to embrace a life of holiness. Having started with the most popular literature about Desert Ascetics, I then use subsequent chapters to problematize the narrative of des-ert monasticism to demonstrate the differences between the religious memory of monasticism and the reality of desert living in late antique Egypt.

In Chapter Three, I examine the fourth century Egyptian monk Antony and his relationship with Bishop Athanasius of Alexandria, who with his *Life of Antony* crafted a saintly rep-utation for Antony as a founder of early monasticism. The chapter is dedicated to Antony because he was considered the quintessential Desert Ascetic. I examine the famous biog-raphy within the broader context of the monastic literature of the Desert Ascetics and the seven letters written by Antony, which are less well known. Together, the sources offer a more nuanced biography of Antony as the role model for Egyptian desert monasticism.

Chapter Four takes up the topic of other Desert Fathers and Mothers. Some appear within the *Sayings,* and others are found in documentary evidence from Egypt, thereby offer-ing a more localized reflection of monasticism than what is found in the Greek and Latin accounts. We will learn that the first monks in Egypt were known by a variety of terms: anchorite (*anachōrētēs*), monk (*monachos*), and renouncer (*apotaktikos*). They practised a technique of training (*askē-sis*), drawing upon the physical and mental discipline known to athletes and philosophers in antiquity. The fourth-century documentary evidence provides a different window into early monasticism and into how we may reread the later sixth-century *Sayings* in light of the new evidence. The exploration of the sources will also highlight how the desert itself was a powerful character in these stories.

In Chapter Five, I introduce the important role of archaeology as a tool to recover the world of the Desert Ascetics in the fifth and sixth centuries. The historical role of archaeology in the study of Christian history was uneven. Initially, Christian archaeology was considered less important than the study of Classical periods. When it was embraced, it was often for the purpose of bolstering theological traditions or theological positions. Part of the difficulty in studying the material remains of early Christian communities is that we now understand that identity, whether religious, gender, or ethnic, is not easily conveyed by or embedded in physical elements as was once thought. Therefore, ascribing identity and ownership to built environments, for example, requires new methodologies of archaeological theory; artifactual evidence must be read with greater sophistication than merely describing an object or site. The methodological foundation described in this chapter helps readers understand what archaeology can and cannot offer in studying the past.

In Chapter Six, I illustrate the importance of looking at the archaeology of places and the built environments of monastic settlements. Extensive archaeological work at the site of Kellia provides important clues about the importance of place for monasticism in Egypt. We will look at excavated materials to gain a greater perspective on what desert monasticism *looked* like. While much of the material dates to the fifth century and later, Kellia provides important correctives to the portrait of monasticism found in the literary sources. The site also enhances the image of monks living in communities, participating in economic activities, and owning *things* that appear in the documentary evidence found in personal archives and recovered from trash mounds.

Chapter Seven takes a deeper dive into the material remains to look at the *realia* of Egyptian monasticism. I use three stories from the *Sayings* to consider the material aspects that are often overlooked as insignificant or serve as tertiary components of the stories. I consider how examining the presence of ovens, bakeries, woven reed mats, and clay statuettes can provide greater context and depth to the literary stories.

In sum, this book is intended to highlight how recent scholarship complicates our portrait of early monasticism in Egypt and to shine a light onto paths of new inquiry in terms of literary, historical, and archaeological evidence for Desert Ascetics.

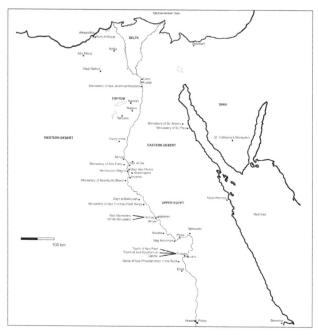

Figure 1. Egyptian sites from the fourth to seventh centuries.
Map: Darlene L. Brooks Hedstrom.

Chapter 1

Desert Ascetics as
Early Christian Celebrities

Who were the Desert Ascetics, and how do they fit into the larger history of the monastic movement? Unlike the early Christian martyrs, whose commitment to Christ was exhibited in the public arenas and courts of the urban landscape, the daily martyrdom of Desert Ascetics was performed on the margins. Ascetics, as soldiers of Christ, moved to the desert to battle against demons both external and internal. They also went to the margins of society to focus on their relationship with God. While Desert Ascetics were *apart* from the world, they were still very much *a part of* the world. Today, we might understand the boldness of their choices as a decision to go "off the grid." But, remarkably, the move to the Egyptian desert was not a fad but a movement that eventually expanded around the globe. Today the movement is known as *monasticism*; one who practices a life apart is known as a *monk*. The early Christian monastic movement focused on being alone with God. Exactly how monks lived out their asceticism differed from person to person, as the movement carried a high level of independence and was not regulated. As time progressed, rules governing monastic life did develop, but not in all communities. The fierce independence of the first monks of Egypt was later celebrated by subsequent generations of monks who regarded the Desert Ascetics as *real* monks. But who were these early Christian heroes?

Desert Ascetics were the first Christian celebrities: their lives were admired with regard to how they ate, how they prayed, how they slept, and how they responded to the challenges of seeking a holy life. Some built tiny homes for shelter in the desert, where they began new lives as servants of God. A small house with a courtyard, a kitchen, a garden, and a place to sleep also served as a place to host visitors who travelled across the Mediterranean simply to see and pray with the famous desert dwellers. Other ascetics clustered their homes together, sometimes living with a few other monks to form larger communities. Together they each helped one other on their personal journeys in mindfulness.

Who Were the Desert Ascetics?

The physical and mental distance from their villages and cities helped monks cultivate a life of self-reflection and total reliance upon God. To prepare for this work, monks trained both their bodies and their minds. The ascetics adopted techniques or training (*askēsis*) in which they limited their diet, divested the bulk of their personal items, and submitted to the authority of a more senior monk. They followed a daily schedule of manual labour or craft production while engaging in prayer. This new life required a level of quietude that could not be found in their previous communities, where societal obligations would draw them away from their commitment to daily martyrdom. They wanted to find a place where they could turn inward, in a very personal way, to engage in regular prayer and meditation.

Very few Desert Ascetics lived alone or in complete isolation. The impetus to relocate to the desert was more about being alone with God than apart from the world. In fact, most monks lived in loose communities with other like-minded monks. Sometimes they lived together in pairs, or in small neighbourhoods, each with their own home. Some monks preferred larger communities, where they lived in dormitories with their own bedrooms, like at a residential college or university. Different forms of community and residential living also fostered a sense of identity for each community. Unlike the forms of monasticism that developed in the western medieval world, where monks became members of particular orders, monasticism in the eastern Mediterranean world was far more eclectic and independent, reflecting the individualism that was a hallmark of monastic communities in regions such as North Africa, Egypt, Palestine, Syria, Anatolia, and Greece.

Desert Ascetics came from all walks of life. Arsenius was a wealthy member of the Byzantine court in Constantinople and brought an enslaved person to care for him while living in Sketis. Arsenius lived in the same community as metalsmith Apelles, gem engraver Macarius, and Apollo, who was accused of murder. Others had worked as farmers or carpenters. Some monks moved to the desert with their families, such as Carion, who brought his son Zacharias to Sketis; others lived with their siblings, such as Ammonios and his two sisters, who settled in separate houses at Nitria. Some Desert Ascetics were wealthy elites who were educated and brought their books with them. They could afford pillows, mattresses, and a change of clothes. Other monks, including formerly enslaved persons, came with nothing and found monastic life a source of stability with secure housing and food. These monks were not educated in reading and writing, but developed revered spiritual wisdom and insight through their practice of memorization and meditation.

Desert Ascetics were primarily Egyptian, but several monks from other regions of the Mediterranean moved to Egypt to live in the new Christian communities. Ancient writers did not always draw attention to the diversity of the ascetics in terms of race and ethnicity. Instead, authors focused more on a monk's remarkable acts of asceticism, such as how long they fasted, the miracles they performed, the spiritual insights they offered, or the humbling lessons they taught. At times, monastic authors did reveal how ascetics were identified by their countries or regions of birth, such as Stephen of Libya, Valens of Palestine, Poseidon of Thebes, Serapion of Egypt, or Evagrius of Pontus. Such naming conventions helped differentiate individuals who shared the same first name or became part of the naming conventions for those who were not native to Egypt. Additionally, Egypt had numerous cities and villages with a long history of diverse populations comprising Egyptian, Greek, Jewish, and Roman communities. Migration into Egypt was common, and legal texts alert us to the fact that people were classified by professions and by their citizenship or place of origin.[1] Markers of difference, such as one's language, skin color, name, or religious practice did not necessarily reveal the mixed heritage that existed throughout Egypt.[2]

Just as monks differed according to class and social status, they also differed according to gender identity. While most of the Desert Ascetics we know by name were identified by others as male, some monks identified as female or gender nonconforming. For example, women such as Sarah and Syncletica were regarded as superior to male monks for their spiritual insights and wisdom, demonstrating how their biographers viewed them as spiritually superior to the men around them. A few individuals, such as Mary of Egypt, are described as having a more fluid gender identity. Exactly how these monks would describe *themselves* is harder to uncover from the sources, which are primarily written by male authors.[3]

---

1 Societies around the Mediterranean often used ethnicity (*ethnos*) to differentiate people instead of race. Ethnicity was determined by where someone held citizenship, where their father was from, or where one was born. Roman census records from Egypt and other papyrological sources help scholars ascertain how individuals were classified and the rights of different ethnic groups. Fischer-Bovet examines how indicators of difference evolved in Egypt from the Ptolemaic to Roman period from a focus upon one's profession to one's citizenship. Since Egypt was a Roman province, the Egyptians as local inhabitants had fewer rights than Romans and Greeks. Christelle Fischer-Bovet, "Official Identity and Ethnicity: Comparing Ptolemaic and Early Roman Egypt," *Journal of Egyptian History* 11, no. 1–2 (2018): 208–42.

2 Gay Byron, *Symbolic Blackness and Ethnic Difference in Early Christian Literature* (New York: Routledge, 2002).

3 Roland Betancourt, *Byzantine Intersectionality: Sexuality, Gender, and*

Some Christian ascetics lived with disabilities and illnesses. Didymus, who became blind while a young child, was a well-respected teacher and theologian in Alexandria, dying when he was eighty-five years old. One female monk lived with mental illness that limited her from participating in the daily routine of her community, but her ascetic discipline was well known and admired. A monk named Elias potentially suffered from a form of Parkinson's, as he experienced tremors, and performed miracles of healing for others, but not himself.[4] In many cases, living with illness or disability was valorized as a reflection of a monk's spiritual piety and strength.

Overall, the Desert Ascetics reflected the diversity of late antique Egypt. Rather than as citizens of an earthly kingdom, monks defined themselves in terms of their heavenly citizenship and dedicated their lives to serving God. As individuals and communities that were self-supporting, monks travelled to villages and cities. Their success quickly became known, and many others wished to see this new life in person, to benefit from the wisdom and healing that the Desert Ascetics offered.

Christianity in Third-Century Egypt

The popularity of desert monasticism is best understood within a larger context of the growing popularity of Christianity in late antique Egypt. Roman Egypt in the third century was home to diverse religious communities. Egyptian religion, with a wide array of local deities from Egypt's pharaonic past, flourished in the homes and villages of the Nile Valley. Temples dedicated to Isis, Sobek, and Serapis, to name just a few, continued to support a wide array of religious activities such as healing shrines, festivals, and prayers for local communities. We learn about the popularity of traditional, native

Race in the Middle Ages (Princeton: Princeton University Press, 2020).

4 Peter Anthony Mena, "Scenting Saintliness: The Ailing Body, Chicana Feminism, and Communal Identity in Ancient Christianity," *Journal of Feminist Studies in Religion* 33, no. 2 (2017): 5–20.

religious practices from archaeological evidence such as amulets, home shrines, funerary markers, "magical" papyri, and letters, in addition to the still-active shrines and temples.

In addition to traditional religious centres, Egypt was also home to Jewish communities, with Alexandria as the heart of the Jewish diaspora. Philo of Alexandria (15 BCE–CE 45) details the multiethnic elements of Egypt's largest city. In subsequent centuries, the Jewish community suffered in the aftermath of Trajan's anti-Jewish policies (CE 115–117). Tensions between the Alexandrian Jewish community and the Roman Alexandrian officials only increased in the third century. We know far less about the Jewish communities outside of Alexandria in late antiquity, as the sources are fewer and archaeological evidence in the first four centuries does not always lend itself to reveal the ethnicity and religious identity of the owners or makers of material remains.

Christianity and the later monastic movement thus developed in a multi-religious landscape. It is not surprising that the story of early Christianity in Egypt is frequently tied to the city of Alexandria, the city where the first leaders of the Christian church emerged. Alexandria is home to the bishop who later became known by the title pope, or *papas*, as a reflection of the authority of the office over all of Egypt.[5] Alexandria was also home to the first Christian school for formal theological training. It was established in the shadow of the great philosophical school of the Serapeum, and the Library of Alexandria. At the catechetical school, Christian teachers such as Clement (ca. 150–ca. 215) and Origen (ca. 180–253) established a popular centre for Christian education shaped by Hellenistic and Roman philosophy and Jewish literature.

In addition to their teaching, Clement and Origen provide us with the main sources for the traditional history of this period. Following them was the historian and bishop Eusebius of Caesarea (260–339). Eusebius's *Ecclesiastical History*

---

5 Stephen J. Davis, *The Early Coptic Papacy: The Egyptian Church and Its Leadership in Late Antiquity* (Cairo: Cairo University Press, 2004), 27–28.

was the first to document the struggles and triumphs of the Christian church. He concluded the *History* with the emperor Constantine and his son Crispus as Christian rulers: "They, having made it their first task to wipe the world clean from hatred of God, rejoiced in the blessing that He had conferred upon them, and, by the thing they did for all men to see, displayed love of virtue and love of God, devotion and thankfulness to the Almighty."[6] For Eusebius, Christianity's triumph over other religious communities was inevitable and swift. However, the reality is that Christianity's relationship to other religions and their worshippers was much more complex, and Christianity only gradually consumed other religious communities over the fifth and sixth centuries.

The third century was a time in which Christians in Egypt and Alexandria solidified their identity as survivors of targeted efforts by the Romans to squelch Christian identity. In 250, Emperor Decius issued an edict to require all residents within his domain to sacrifice to the Roman gods. The fact that Christians did not sacrifice to the Roman gods clearly indicated a separate identity and lack of support for the Roman authorities. Decius' edict required all residents to sacrifice in the presence of a Roman official. The individual was then issued official proof of having completed the sacrifice in the form of a certificate (Latin *libellus*). Many of these *libelli* survive from Egypt and demonstrate the importance of having "proof" of one's adherence to the law. Christians in Egypt and elsewhere were faced with a choice: assimilate back into the dominant religious activities or refuse to participate and face criminal charges and death. Naturally, other options emerged, such as running away into "self-exile" or having someone sacrifice on your behalf in order to acquire a legal certificate. Decius's edict was a threat to Christians, but it was also an attempt by the imperial court to try to regulate and standardize traditional religious practices more

---

6 Eusebius, *The Ecclesiastical History*, bk. 10, chap. 9, cited from Kirsopp Lake, J. E. L. Oulton, H. J. Lawlor, and William Heinemann, eds., 2 vols. (London: Putnam, 1926–1932).

widely. The edict's ability to enforce any empire-wide regulation failed in the end, and native religious practices continued to flourish, along with Christian communities.

Christianity in Fourth-Century Egypt

Christianity in Egypt in the fourth century is marked by four components: survival from the last and most significant persecution, the careers of charismatic bishops, internal Christian controversies, and the rise of monasticism. All four components are interrelated, as they helped shape the Egyptian church, its importance as a centre for what may be called proto-Orthodoxy, and the backdrop for the monastic movement.

The last attempt by the Roman emperors to either assimilate or eliminate Christian communities altogether came at the beginning of the fourth century. At that time, Emperors Diocletian, Galerius, and Maximin (from 303 to 313) required all inhabitants to publicly declare subservience to the emperor and the imperial cult. The "Great Persecution," as it is known, was particularly active in Egypt and specifically in Alexandria. Stories of the martyrs from Egypt appear in the pages of Eusebius (e.g., bk. 8, chap. 8) in which he describes in detail the various forms of torture and eventual death ordered by the Roman officials. For the Egyptian church, the period of Christian martyrdom was formally marked by the first year of Diocletian's reign in 284 as the dawn of a new age and eventually would become known as the "Era of the Martyrs" and be used as a perpetual reminder of the resiliency of the Christians.

Alexandrian bishops played an important role in shaping Egyptian Christianity, but Christian historians, like Eusebius and others, started to view Alexandrian Christianity as differing from that of Egypt proper. A binary emerged whereby Alexandrian Christianity was defined by the catechetical school and the increasing popularity and teachings of the Bishop of Alexandria. The central figure of fourth-century Alexandria was Bishop Athanasius (ca. 295/9–373), who was the patriarch of Alexandria for forty-five years. He attended the Council of Nicaea in 325 as the secretary to Bishop Alexander and was appointed Alexander's successor upon his death in 328. Athanasius's commitment to root out heretical teachings, particularly those of Arius, and his run-ins with various emperors created a colourful career for the bishop. Regardless of whether one views Athanasius as a heroic defender of orthodoxy or a persistent politician, one cannot define Egyptian Christianity without him.

Athanasius also played a pivotal role in the monastic movement, as the author of the first biography of a Desert Ascetic named Antony who died in 356. The *Life of Antony* was an immediate success, and was soon translated from Greek into Latin. The *Life of Antony* was the first biography of a Christian outside of the New Testament, and followed earlier models of lives of famous philosophers such as the Neoplatonic teachers Plotinus and Porphyry, also residents of Alexandria. The *Life* did more than record Antony's existence: it offered a model—implicitly approved by Athanasius, the Bishop of Alexandria, for how other Christian men and women could adopt a life dedicated to asceticism.

The popularity of Antony, and others like him, gained the attention of like-minded Christians from North Africa, Rome, Constantinople, and Jerusalem. By the end of the fourth century, famous Christian authors such as Jerome, John Cassian, Rufinus, and Evagrius visited Egypt, and the Desert Ascetics in particular. Some of these travellers wrote accounts of their experiences in letters to others, as instructional guides, or in reports of their time spent in desert communities. John Cassian wrote his *Conferences* and *Institutes* as manuals for his fellow monks in Gaul, after he had lived for several years at Kellia. His works are often consulted as reflections upon his lived experience in the Egyptian desert. Similarly, Palladius is frequently invoked as a witness to the Desert Ascetics for his biographical collection of monks, both male and female, in the *Lausiac History*. These accounts helped promote Egyptian monasticism as an important feature of Egyptian Christianity and elevated Desert Ascetics like Antony to become known throughout the Christian world.

After Eusebius wrote the *Ecclesiastical History*, other writers produced extended histories that continued where Eusebius left off. Rufinus, for example, translated Eusebius' history into Latin and then added two chapters to bring the history up to date, covering the years 325 to 395. Written for a colleague in Latin-speaking Aquileia, Rufinus provided brief discussions of the Desert Ascetics, which helped foster a western perception of Egyptian desert monasticism. Rufinus, who had lived in Egypt as a monk in the deserts of the Delta, wanted his readers to know "those who dwelt throughout the great desert and worked the signs and wonders of the apostles in simplicity of life and sincerity of heart."[7] Rufinus refers to Antony as the "first desert-dweller" and describes the desert of Nitria as home to the "fathers of the monks" (*History of the Church*, bk. 11, chap. 4). He mentions some monks by name, such as Macarius of the upper desert, Macarius of the lower desert; Isidore of Sketis, Pambo of Kellia, and Moses and Benjamin of Nitria. He also alludes to other stories about Desert Ascetics that are less well known and have "escaped the notice of those far removed from them" (*History of the Church*, bk. 10, chap. 8). Unfortunately, Rufinus never provided the tantalizing details in his final publication.

Later Church historian Socrates of Constantinople (ca. 380–439) produced an expanded Greek version of the *Ecclesiastical History*, covering the years 324 to 439, improving upon the work of Eusebius and Rufinus. Socrates discusses monasticism in general by highlighting prominent leaders in desert monasticism and the role of Egyptian monks in directing the movement through their devotion and healing miracles. Socrates's work inspired two other historians, Sozomen (ca. 400–445) and Theodoret of Cyrrhus (393–460), to write revised church histories. Sozomen's history compiles existing popular literature and allows us to see an emerging narrative of monastic origins and the place of desert monasticism

---

[7] *History of the Church*, bk. 11, chap. 8. Cited from Rufinus of Aquileia, *History of the Church*, trans. Philip R. Amidon (Washington, DC: The Catholic University of America Press, 2016), 444.

before the publication of the *Sayings* in their various forms. By the time Theodoret of Cyrrhus wrote his survey called *Religious History* (ca. 450), he included accounts of Syrian monks and the Desert Ascetics of Egypt. Read collectively, the ecclesiastical histories above illustrate the evolving narrative of how monasticism began and the place of Desert Ascetics in the overall history of monasticism.

Conclusion

In the third and fourth centuries, more and more men and women elected to pursue alternatives to the social expectations of marriage and to become agents of their own lives. The strong independence of the first Desert Ascetics offered a model for how Christians could inhabit the world on their own terms. By physically moving to the margins, Desert Ascetics removed themselves from the entanglements of local communities to pursue the solitary path toward continual engagement with God. They were living the angelic life, and their new homes were battlefields where they fought demons, their own bodies, and the spiritual temptation to return to the comfort of their families. It was not an easy life in the desert. Only those with a steadfast focus could succeed in the new endeavour.

Chapter 2

What Did the Desert Ascetics Teach and How Did They Live?

The Desert Ascetics became the modern pop stars of their day. Christians from around the Eastern Mediterranean wanted to meet these extraordinary Christians and see if everything about them was true. They wanted to discover what blessings or miracles could be achieved by being near the living angels of God. In the end, the solitude monks desired was replaced by the noise of larger monastic communities and a stream of visitors: local and foreign, monastic and nonmonastic. The world, with all its entanglements, came to the desert, and the boundaries between an idealized desert utopia and the noisy world started to fade. But, the memories of the Desert Ascetics remained, as did the questions about them. Who were they? What did they teach? How did they live? How could they help other Christians?

In this chapter, I use the late fifth- and early sixth-century collections of the *Sayings of the Desert Fathers and Mothers* as a starting point to sketch out the identity of the Desert Ascetics. The stories in the *Sayings* were written down at least one hundred to one hundred and fifty years after the lives of the individuals they purport to describe. The *Sayings* are not eyewitness accounts of the first Desert Fathers and Mothers but are later accounts of the first generations of desert monasticism. While some scholars in the past have explored how the *Sayings* reflect and retain the oral tradition and oral histories of fourth-century Egyptian monasticism, I adopt the more moderate view that the *Sayings* reflect the world of the later generations of the fifth and sixth-century monks rather than serving as a window into the fourth century. Even with a conservative view of the historicity of the *Sayings*, we can still learn a great deal about how later generations reflected upon and constructed a history of desert monks and the deserts in which they lived.

What Are the *Sayings*?

The *Sayings* exist largely in three main collections. The first, the *Alphabetical* collection, comprises a series of stories organized by the names of the monks in alphabetical order, running from Antony to Zeno. The second collection is the *Systematic* collection, in which stories are arranged by topics, such as self-control, humility, discretion, and a state of calm or profound peace known in Greek as *hēsychia*. The *Systematic* collection serves as a monastic how-to guide to help monks address specific concerns and challenges of daily living. The sections on hospitality and forbearance, for instance, include stories about the complications that come with learning and living with others. The third collection is known as the *Anonymous* collection, in which most of the monks in the stories are not named and only referred to as "father" (*Abba*) or as "elder man" (*gerōn*). Within the *Anonymous* collection are additional stories that may reference named monks known from the *Systematic* and *Alphabetical* collections.

The teachings found in three collections range from spiritual reflections on God to the need for discipline and humility to the daily struggles of living as a monk. The *Systematic* collection of the *Sayings* conveniently offers a manual for monks. It gathers some of the *Alphabetic* and *Anonymous Sayings* and creates a thematic order. The ancient monastic editors to the *Systematic Sayings* explain in the *Prologue* that it was too difficult to remember the teachings, which were not presented in an order that was conducive for easy recall. The division of the sayings into twenty-one thematic chapters fostered better memorization. The volume is intended to "[S]chool those who are desirous of successfully pursuing the

Figure 2. *Apophthegmata Patrum*, Sahidic Coptic. Vienna, Österreichische Nationalbibliothek, P.Vindob., K321b verso. Used with the kind permission of the Österreichische Nationalbibliothek, Papyrussammlung & Papyrusmuseum.

heavenly way of life and willing to travel the road to the king-dom of heaven by emulating and imitation them" (*AP.S.* Pro-logue 1: *Book of Elders*, trans. Wortley, 3). The idea of imita-tion was important. Using the first monks from the Egyptian deserts as models for *how* to live the monastic life allowed later monks to have a template for tailoring their own goals for a successful ascetic life.

In looking at all the *Sayings*, we learn the names of one hundred and seventeen male monks and three female monks. Antony is the most recognized monk in the list of male monks, even though he did not live in the great deserts of Nitria, Kellia, or Sketis, but by the Red Sea. Monks from other parts of the Mediterranean appear in the fuller list of famous monks, including Basil the Great from Cappadocia and John Cassian, who established monasteries in Gaul. Most of the monks were men who trained in the Egyptian desert communities, and a chain of authority emerged whereby famous teachers and their students became role models for Christian living.

What Is the Desert?

It is important to have some knowledge of Egypt's geography in order for us to ground the stories of the Desert Ascetics in the actual, material landscape rather than the mytholo-gized landscape that emerges from the written accounts. An orientation to geography will also help us understand where and what the desert is that was home to the Desert Ascetics. Geography will also help us understand the regional limits of those locations—something not clarified in the *Sayings of the Desert Fathers and Mothers*.

The majority of the Desert Ascetics are associated with the deserts that dot the marshy Delta in northern Egypt. The Delta sits atop a high-water table, allowing communi-ties to easily irrigate fields and create wells, even in sand. Most of this area was used for settlements, but archaeolog-ical work in the Delta in earlier periods was limited because the sites flooded during excavation. Today, the landscape is heavily controlled by irrigation systems and desert reclamation efforts, making it easier for archaeologists to recover evidence of forgotten settlements. Efforts in the twentieth century identified the locations of three of the most famous monastic centres: Nitria, Kellia, and Sketis.

Nitria was established by Amoun and known in Coptic as Pernouj. It was a popular first destination for new monks and visitors to Egypt and was considered the earliest site of monasticism in northern Egypt. It is associated with the modern village of al-Barnuji and has yet to be excavated. Kellia, meanwhile, was initially developed as a satellite retreat from the hustle and bustle of Nitria. But Kellia soon surpassed Nitria and became an important centre for monastic education and Christian visitors. When the noise and size of Kellia became too great, Pherme was settled as a smaller satellite settlement where monks could find a respite from the demands of public life at Kellia. All three settlements were abandoned by the eighth and ninth centuries.

Sketis, on the other hand, continued to be a centre of monasticism and is currently home to four thriving Coptic monasteries: the Monastery of St. Baramous, the Monastery of the Syrians, the Monastery of St. Bishoi, and the Monastery of St. Macarius. The monasteries are distributed in an area known today as Wadi al-Natrun, a name that refers to the alkaline lakes that provided the necessary natron for ancient embalming. The continuing presence of monastic communities at Sketis makes the region one of the oldest monastic communities in Egypt, along with the monasteries of St. Antony and St. Paul by the Red Sea.

Moving south from the Delta is the Nile Valley proper, which has a tripartite landscape: the Nile Valley with its agricultural fields, the *outer* desert on the edges of the fields, and the *inner* desert, which includes the Eastern Desert (leading to the Red Sea) and the Western Desert (leading to the oases). The Nile provided the most efficient and accessible form of transportation through Egypt. On either side of the Nile are agricultural floodplains which, before the construction of the Aswan dam, regularly flooded, providing Egyptians with sta-

Figure 3. East bank of the Nile showing the visible agricultural fields and the close proximity of the Outer Desert. The Inner Desert is beyond the horizon and much further from the Nile Valley and village settlements. Minya, Egypt.
Photo: Darlene L. Brooks Hedstrom.

ble seasonal harvests. Beyond the cultivated plains are limestone cliffs of the *outer* desert, which box in the river and the agricultural fields. The cliffs and the sand that accumulates around them contrast with the green cultivated fields below.

The *outer* desert contained ancient Egyptian tombs whose openings could be seen even from the Nile. Quarrymen and soldiers spent time in the outer desert and sometimes spent the night there in caves or in "open" tombs, whose doors were no longer present. Monks, like the soldiers and quarrymen, discovered that the *outer* desert could provide accessible housing "away" from the village but still nearby. The *outer* desert was part of the inhabited world, whereas the *inner* desert was not. The *inner* desert was located beyond the horizon (if you looked at the landscape from the Nile or the agricultural lands), and thus the *inner* desert lay beyond the outer desert. The difference between the two deserts was significant to late antique people. At the beginning of the

Figure 4. Doorways for open pharaonic tombs at
Dayr al-Dik in Minya, Egypt.
Photo: Darlene L. Brooks Hedstrom.

Life of Antony, Athanasius lets his readers know that monks
were living primarily in the *outer* desert, and nobody had yet
moved to the *inner* desert. It would take someone coura-
geous, like Antony, to venture into the unknown landscape of
the *inner* desert. As the monastic movement evolved, monks
who could tolerate and thrive in the *inner* desert were used
as models to inspire others to move from the comfort of the
outer desert to remote desert locations.

What Did They Teach?

The *Sayings* highlight several aspects of monastic life. With so
many stories, however, it was sometimes difficult for monks
to find the appropriate guidance they needed. The *Systematic*
collection was created to provide a topical index of monastic teachings. Of the twenty-one themes of the *Systematic*
collection, four themes illustrate the ways in which monks

pursued holiness by learning from their elders and reflecting on essential goals for shifting one's focus from the self to God alone. The four examples include perfection, discretion, watchfulness, and humility.

Monastic perfection was a central concern for monks. The first chapter of the *Systematic Sayings* includes thirty-seven stories detailing techniques for cultivating a life of perfection with monks whose ascetic life was a role model for others. For instance, Antony said: "Always have God before your eyes wherever you go...have the testimony from Holy Scriptures [and]...do not be in a hurry to move away" (*AP.S.* 1.1: *Book of Elders*, trans. Wortley, 7). Abba Sisoes advised monks to "cast your will behind you, do not worry yourself [see Matt 6:25] about the concerns of the world" in order to find peace (*AP.S.* 1.26: *Book of Elders*, trans. Wortley, 12). Those seeking a more practical path to perfection were told "eat hay, wear hay, sleep on hay, and acquire a heart of steel" (*AP.S.* 1.28: *Book of Elders*, trans. Wortley, 12). Such sayings demonstrate the wide range of instructions for monastic living.

Part of the journey to perfection included a monk's attention to discretion. The tenth chapter of the *Systematic Sayings* includes 194 sayings on discretion, which range from one-line statements to complex stories. The number of sayings on this topic points to the importance of cultivating discretion and the challenges monks encountered in developing the habit. The axioms for discretion include: "Knowledge of God is sufficient for the health of the soul" and "The truly wise one is not the one who teaches by word but he who educates by deed" (*AP.S.* 10.109 and 10.141: *Book of Elders*, trans. Wortley, 170 and 177). These examples illustrate how discretion could be experienced on a personal and public level. Even if monks lived more independently or with a few monks in their homes, they still encountered other monks and were thus bound to compare their own ascetic practice to that of another. It was, therefore, important to be cautious and to practise discretion when meeting others because a monk may say "one thing and wickedly [have] another in his heart" (*AP.S.* 10.30: *Book of Elders*, trans. Wortley, 150). Monitoring one's behaviour, then, was just as important as monitoring the behaviour of another.

Watchfulness was another topic that helped monks pursue perfection and to develop discretion. Like perfection, the art of watchfulness was difficult to attain. In one story, a monk asked his teacher Abba Sisoes: "I want to keep a watch on my heart, but I am not able." Abba Sisoes responded by asking: "How are we to keep a watch on the heart when the door to our tongue lies open?" (*AP.S.* 11.67: *Book of Elders*, trans. Wortley, 203). Each day was, according to Sisoes, an opportunity to start anew. The daily assessment involved practising silence, allowing anxious thoughts to come without engaging, meditating with fear of God, and having hope in one's ability to defeat temptations. A monk could also maintain watchfulness by envisioning themselves as celestial beings: "A monk ought to be all eyes, like the cherubim and seraphim" (*AP.S.* 11.15: *Book of Elders*, trans. Wortley, 191). On a more practical level, monks were taught to adopt "piety, decency, simplicity, gentleness, and respect for all folk" (*AP.S.* 11.54: Book of Elders, trans. Wortley, 201). By watching one's thoughts, speech, and behaviour, monks could make progress toward perfection and keep their eyes turned toward God.

Humility, found in the fifteenth chapter of the *Systematic Sayings*, is a topic that recognizes the complexities of pursuing perfection, discretion, and watchfulness. A monk could easily become boastful and judgemental without a humble heart. An elder monk explained to his disciples: "Be of a mind...before all else not to trust your own ideas at all...humble yourself before the brothers and cut your own will off from yourself. If one of them insults you or another afflicts you some day, pray for him as though he were performing great things for you" (*AP.S.* 15.136: *Book of Elders*, trans. Wortley, 288). Monks were taught to limit their speech and quiet their minds. In some cases, monks needed to break their will and pride; this was a process that required brutal honesty and erosion of one's self-worth. For example, an elder explained humility as "thinking that you are more sinful than all other folk and despising yourself as one who does no good thing in the sight of God" (*AP.S.* 15.26: *Book of Elders*, trans. Wortley, 254). Considering oneself as inferior to others was a technique for diminishing a sense of superiority—it was better to "pay attention not to the sins of others but always to one's own" (*AP.S.* 15.103: *Book of Elders*, trans. Wortley, 272). Practising humility was thought to be a spiritual counterweight to the coexistent need to pursue perfection, watchfulness, and discretion.

The wide array of teachings on monitoring one's own life and flourishing in a community with others demonstrates the popularity of the diverse collections of the *Sayings of the Desert Fathers and Mothers*. Rather than focusing on a monk's prior life, the *Sayings* address the very important task of navigating daily life. Abba Motios advised a brother to "not seek to be known for anything special" and to "follow the same manner of life as everyone else" (Motios 1: *Give Me a Word*, trans. Wortley, 204). The *Sayings* demonstrate that even with excellent role models for ascetic living, the most practical advice was to do your best and to live in a community with others.

Daily Life of the Desert Ascetics

The *Sayings* offer very few details about how individuals came to adopt desert monasticism. When we are introduced to Desert Ascetics, they are already well-established in their life in the desert. We learn that most monks lived in houses, caves, or simple buildings with one or two others. They visited others and hosted guests. On weekends, they gathered with others in the area to celebrate the Eucharist and share food.

The Desert Ascetics differed from monks who lived in larger communities and were known as coenobites—coenobites shared common living spaces, eating areas, and abided by a hierarchy of monastic authority. In the south, for example, Pachomius established a cluster of monasteries that used house groups with a supervisor to organize monks under the authority of one chief monastic leader. Communal or coenobitic living offered monks clear expectations for when to pray, eat, sleep, and work, because they carried out such duties together.[1] While the *Sayings* do include some teachings from coenobitic monks, such as Pachomius, they are not often included in the collections, as the bulk of the stories recounts examples of monks living independently in desert places such as Kellia, Sketis, and Nitria in northern Egypt. Embedded within the various stories and statements, we can find aspects of how monks lived in the desert. Examining *how* the monks lived day-to-day will illustrate that desert living was not as solitary as scholars once believed and that Desert Ascetics were engaged with local communities even as they maintained a high degree of independence.

As reflected in the *Sayings*, the flexibility of life in the desert was part of the appeal for those seeking a monastic life more tailored than what was found in the structured settlements in central and southern Egypt. Three monks may have lived together, but each one may have adopted a different eating schedule, time for prayer, and form of manual labour. What tied them together was not their schedules or methods but their mutual desire for perfection, biblical education, and their shared pursuit of closeness with God. Living as a spiritual assistant to an older monk allowed those with less experience to learn by example and discover the ascetic disciplines that best suited their needs.

One way to keep temptations and disruptions at bay during the week was by doing manual labour. Working with one's hands and making things provided a useful way to mark time, demonstrating the principle that "unless one work(s), he does not get a reward from God" (Isaiah 5: *Give Me a Word*, trans. Wortley, 112). Basket-making was a widespread form of work, consisting of braiding cords from palm fronds and then stitching the coils together to form the basket. The work also allowed for deep concentration and prayer. John the Little's meditation was so focused on one occasion that he stitched together two baskets into one (John the Little 11:

---

1 For an overview of monasticism in southern Egypt where monks were assembled in a more communal structure see Rousseau, *Pachomius*, 57–76.

Give Me a Word, trans. Wortley, 133). Monastic baskets were sold in the villages to acquire necessities like bread and other provisions for monks living alone. Baskets were also always in need as they served several functions. Monks used baskets to hold bread, fruit, tiles, and even sand. Monks also wove mats that could serve many functions, such as surfaces for sleeping, places to sit, and pillows. A few monks were also known to wear mats as clothing in order to train their bodies not to desire comfort. Braiding ropes, too, provided an opportunity to focus one's thoughts and hands in the process of making. Even the great Antony found that braiding ropes and prayer helped to alleviate his low feelings and to bring him joy (Antony 1: *Give Me a Word*, trans. Wortley, 31). Working was also a means of being self-sufficient, and not relying on charity. Having a sense of purpose during the day also equipped monks to resist the temptation to sleep at all hours and to seek out others for gossip.

The evening was often the time for monks to practise the "little" *synaxis,* which consisted of reciting or reading Psalms and prayer. Isidore of Sketis was known for performing his *synaxis* day and night (Isidore 4: *Give Me a Word*, trans. Wortley, 144). Arsenius did not allow himself any water until he had completed his evening *synaxis* (Arsenius 24: *Give Me a Word*, trans. Wortley, 44). Sometimes a few monks gathered together to recite, read, and pray for a shared *synaxis* during the week. After eating, monks would sleep either in their rooms on mats or out in the open, in a courtyard or on the roofs of their dwellings. When morning came, the daily cycle began again.

During the weekend, monks met to celebrate the Eucharist, share stories from the past week, and encourage each other about the week ahead. Missing the gathering could be an indication that a monk was suffering or struggling with their monastic practice. Monks wore special garments or their best clothes for the weekend gatherings, as they joined the angels in celebrating the holy Eucharist. It was surprising, therefore, when Theodore of Pherme appeared for the gathering in an old torn, and tattered garment. Such clothing would be unacceptable for others, but the *Sayings* explain that he was robbed once of his belongings, and he offered to tear his garment in half so that the robbers would not leave him without something to wear to the service (Theodore of Pherme 29: *Give Me a Word*, trans. Wortley, 123). Despite the poor quality of his clothes, Theodore's dedication to being present at the gathering was a lesson for all monks to do whatever was necessary to attend the Eucharist. After the liturgical gathering, monks would eat together or receive food to take back to their homes and begin the work week restored.

Conclusion

The three collections of the *Sayings of the Desert Fathers and Mothers* include memorable stories that reflected concerns of practical ascetic living and the more intangible search for oneness with God. Both Rabbinic and Classical literature used similar pronouncements and stories, known as *chreiai*, to teach their communities revealing how Christian monastic literature developed in a diverse literary world.[2] The use of stories linked to a particular speaker also reveals various modes for monitoring correct behaviour and correction. The popularity of such ideas in Egypt may reach further back to the wisdom literature or instructions of the Greco-Roman period. As tales of how to inhabit the world, the *Sayings* allow us to see what late fifth-century and early sixth-century monks wanted to impart to others. Subsequent generations adopted the *Sayings* as historical accounts and, later, historians did the same. Now, with greater attention to reception history, transmission history, and the influx of less utilized sources from the same period, we can better understand how the mythology of the Desert Ascetics was set in motion.

---

2 Michal Bar-Asher Siegal, *Early Christian Monastic Literature and the Babylonian Talmud* (Cambridge: Cambridge University Press, 2013).

Chapter 3

Who Was the First Desert Ascetic?

Antony of Egypt (251–356) was Egypt's most revered and celebrated monk. Considered the premier Desert Ascetic, Antony appears throughout monastic and Christian literature as a founder of the monastic movement, even though other Christians were already practising asceticism and living alone on the borders of Egyptian villages. Although Antony is not technically the first Desert Ascetic, he is considered the most recognized of the Desert Fathers.

Antony appears in 119 stories in the various collections, with thirty-eight sayings containing specific teachings attributed to him in the *Alphabetic Sayings*. The remaining eighty-one references illustrate the ways in which Antony legitimized the words or practices of other monks. We observe how his name builds the authority of others simply through association. In this chapter, I examine the life and memory of Antony of Egypt, whose story towers over all others in the *Sayings*.

We will examine three different sources: seven letters Antony wrote in Coptic; a Greek biography of Antony written by Athanasius (d. 373), Bishop of Alexandria; and the *Sayings* and other monastic stories that profile Antony. The Coptic letters are perhaps the least well-known of the three sources because, for many years, scholars questioned their authenticity and disregarded the letters as a source for early desert monasticism. Instead, Antony is known chiefly through Athanasius's highly celebrated biography, the *Life of Antony,* written shortly after the monk's death in the mid-fourth century. The biography became a best seller and was soon translated from Greek into many other languages. The biography made Antony the most famous of the Desert Ascetics, and his reputation was further augmented by his appearance in the fifth- and sixth-century *Sayings*. We will look at the sources, in turn, to examine how Antony emerged as the first and most significant of the Desert Ascetics.

Antony the Letter Writer

Antony wrote seven undated letters to monastic communities under his care and direction. The letters were first written in Coptic; later copies exist in Arabic, Georgian, Latin, and Syriac. Although we do not possess any copies of the letters in Greek, the later Syriac and Georgian letters exhibit philological elements that reveal that they were based on earlier Greek manuscripts. Thus, the diverse corpus of Antony's letters demonstrates the continued importance of his correspondence for later generations.

Scholars have known about Antony's letters since Jerome first referenced them in 392. But their existence moved into the background in light of Athanasius' biography, which stressed that Antony was uneducated. In analyzing the sources about Antony and his later memory in subsequent monastic sources, Samuel Rubenson makes a compelling case for the authenticity of the letters and their importance for understanding Antony and early monasticism.[1] Rubenson's work also highlights the overreliance on Athanasius's *Life of Antony* and the need to build a more nuanced portrait of the first monastic leader.

Modelling his letters after the New Testament writer Paul, Antony writes with affection and concern for his beloved brothers. Antony crafts complex pastoral messages to encourage monks to stay focused on living a holy life. He highlights the importance of salvation, the humility needed

---

[1] Rubenson, *Letters of Antony*, 35–47.

to accept the Spirit's call, and the centrality of Trinitarian belief (Letter 5: Rubenson, *Letters of Antony*, 212–15). Antony knows his Bible well and frequently cites the Old and New Testaments. He also alludes to ideas found in the teachings of Origen, a controversial Christian Alexandrian teacher whose ideas were later expunged from monastic literature. The only contemporary person Antony mentions by name is Arius, a fourth-century presbyter who taught that Jesus was subordinate to God the Father. Arius's teachings were popular but were considered heretical by his chief opponent, Bishop Athanasius. Antony does not condemn Arius but rather expresses disagreement and disappointment. He warns his fellow monks to be alert and cautious, especially about Arius's "strange words," and the "an unhealable wound" he has created within the Christian community (Letter 4: Rubenson, *Letters of Antony*, 210–11).

Antony is most concerned in the letters with personal piety, faithfulness, and self-reflection, and much less so on larger theological and ecclesiastical conflicts in Alexandria. He elevates the importance of knowledge—*gnōsis*—of God over everything else. He also speaks of a genderless spiritual essence—*ousia* (Letters 3 and 6: Rubenson, *Letters of Antony*, 206–9, 216–24). Antony's philosophical tone reflects his comfort with speaking about the spirit, mind, essence, and heart as parts of an individual whom God created. He urges his audience not to be tempted by complacency but rather to be alert and prepared to have their hearts and lives assessed (Letters 2, 6, and 7: Rubenson, *Letters of Antony*, 203–5; 216–31).

Only one letter addresses modes of practical living. In Letter 1, Antony encourages monks to fast and to hold vigils (Letter 1: Rubenson, *Letters of Antony*, 197–202). He stresses the importance of limiting desire, including sexual desire, and unnecessary speech, eating, and work. These practical instructions are balanced by encouragement to study the word of God, pray often, and renounce the world and its physical things. Letter 5 echoes, if briefly, the call to reject earthly possessions and to renounce them.

In the end, Antony's letters demonstrate his compassion and conviction for his fellow monastic brothers. With a pastoral tone, he encourages the monks to be attuned to the complex relationship between their bodies and spirits in their preparation for the next life. He employs scripture and ideas from other Christian teachers, such as Origen, to persuade his audience to be faithful followers of Jesus. The letters illustrate that Antony does not regard himself as a founder of a new monastic movement. Instead, his letters reveal a man aware that he is a teacher of Christian living and focused on guiding others who are not remarkable except in that they share a similar pursuit of ascetic living.

Antony in Athanasius's *Life of Antony* ca. 358

For Athanasius, Antony is the monk to emulate. In contrast to his letters, where Antony is a philosophizing teacher, Athanasius's Antony is a trailblazing star of ascetic virtue, orthodox theology, and spiritual wisdom. Written only a few years after Antony's death, the *Life of Antony* provides an engaging account of one of Egypt's earliest Desert Ascetics. The biography contains drama, miracles, tips for ascetic living, and a clear defence of Alexandrian theology. Although Athanasius purports to have had a close relationship with Antony during the monk's life, most scholars are skeptical of this claim.

In the Preface to the *Life*, Athanasius addresses an unspecified group of monks who wish to learn more about how Antony lived.[2] Athanasius leads the reader to believe that within Antony's lifetime, the monk's reputation for holy and ascetic living was already gaining enough attention that he, Athanasius, was required to set the record straight about what Antony was doing in the desert. Athanasius wants to present an ascetic life that others could imitate. Furthermore, Athanasius positions himself as the transmitter of a

---

2 Pref. 2: Athanasius, *Life of Antony*, trans. Vivian and Athanassakis, 50–55.

trustworthy and reliable account of Christian asceticism.[3] Rather than from Antony as a direct source, Athanasius likely gained information about the monk from one of Antony's successors, Abba Serapion, who later became Bishop Serapion of Thmuis (d. ca. 360).

The biography relates that Antony was a wealthy young man before he became the ultimate ascetic. Orphaned at age twenty, Antony was a rich young adult responsible for his younger sister and for the property he inherited. He disposed of his estate and moveable property after hearing Jesus's words in a sermon at a local church: "If you wish to be perfect, go, sell your possessions, and give the money to the poor, and you will have treasure in heaven; then come, follow me" (Matthew 19:21). Compelled by this message, Antony lived in self-imposed poverty, and since "no monk knew at all the remote desert," he moved to a location not far from his village to live with an older man already practising monasticism (Athanasius, *Life of Antony*, 3: trans. Vivian and Athanassakis, 61–63).

Like Antony, Christians who wanted to live an ascetic life had two choices, which depended greatly upon one's gender. Women could join a group of "faithful virgins." Antony, who had a younger sister, relocated her to such a group. Athanasius does not discuss whether she had a say in this decision.[4] Men, meanwhile, had many more options as they could take up residency on the edge of a property, live in an abandoned tomb or quarry, remodel a natural cave, or even refurbish an abandoned building. Women were not afforded the same freedom of independent housing. While some women resided in the deserts, monastic women were often associated with small communities in cities and towns and lived with other

---

3 David Brakke, *Athanasius and Asceticism* (Baltimore: Johns Hopkins University Press, 1998), 206–10.

4 *Life of Antony*, 3: trans. Vivian and Athanassakis, 61–63. Athanasius tells his readers little about Antony's sister, although Antony did see her once more at the end of her life.

single or widowed women. Athanasius describes all of these spaces as monasteries. Small, intimate, and not equipped to house many individuals, the new monastic homes showed great variety.

Antony followed the model of seeking out others to live with before venturing into asceticism on his own. Not much is known of the unnamed monks that Antony found, but it is important to note that Antony had many ascetic resources to turn to as he was starting out. His monasticism was like others'—independent and local. Athanasius tells his readers that Antony is like a honeybee going from monk to monk, offering and receiving the nectar of wisdom wherever he travelled.

After an unspecified time spent battling demons, observing fasts, praying continually, and sleeping very little, Antony wanted a change. He decided it was time to move away from his village outpost and head up to a tomb outside his village (*Life of Antony*, 8: trans. Vivian and Athanassakis, 76–79). Athanasius is vague on the exact place, but it must have been known to others, since Antony made prior arrangements with one of his friends to bring bread to him every few days. The tomb was like hundreds of other pharaonic tombs visible from the Nile and the riverbanks (see figure 4 above). It was common for seasonal workers to inhabit tombs and quarries. When the original tomb doors disappeared, it was easy to add a door from the inside and convert the space for daily living. The conversion of rupestrian, or rock-hewn, spaces into dwellings was a long-practised skill in Egypt, both in the ancient and modern periods.[5]

Some Christians, perhaps inspired by Antony's story, transformed quarries and caves into chapels or, in rare cases, churches. Such spaces served as places for liturgical activities for nearby monks and other Christians living further out in the inner desert. Although the reused spaces at Dayr al-Dik, for example, do not date as early as the time

---

5 Kees van der Spek, *The Modern Neighbors of Tutankhamun: History, Life, and Work in the Villages of the Theban West Bank* (Cairo: The American University in Cairo, 2011), 157–70.

Figure 5. Painted niche for a chapel or church in a quarried room at Dayr al-Dik in Minya, Egypt. Photo: Darlene L. Brooks Hedstrom.

of Antony, one chapel, with a carved apse and painted programme, allows us to visualize the skills and techniques used for recrafting a quarry into a space for Christian worship. Antony's reclamation of a tomb for a dwelling, then, was not out of the ordinary. What was different, according to Athanasius, was what happened to Antony *inside* the tomb.

Antony was not faring well in the tomb, and when a friend brought him bread, he found the young monk lying on the floor as if dead. Thinking that Antony had died, the friend carried him back to the village church, where villagers and relatives gathered to prepare for a funeral. However, Antony awoke while all the people slept around him. He convinced his friend to help him return to the tomb without waking the others. The second internment in the tomb became one of Athanasius's most referenced scenes from the *Life*. Restored and determined to start again, Antony was now ready for intense spiritual combat with demons, an epic battle that became a popular theme in art from the medieval period onwards, depicted in paintings by Michelangelo, El Greco, Salvador Dali, and others.

Figure 6. Michelangelo, *Torment of Saint Antony*, ca. 1487. Kimbell Art Museum, Fort Worth, Texas. Used with kind permission of the Kimbell Art Museum.

Antony passed the test of his asceticism and established his commitment to serve God. Energized by this test, he decided to move further away from the village and his community to a deserted building, usually identified as an abandoned barracks or fortress, most likely made of mud bricks. Athanasius emphasizes that Antony was now more alone and secluded than he had been previously. But this separation from the world was not as pronounced as it may sound. Antony, to them, seemed like an ancient Henry David Thoreau, who was considered a hermit at Walden Pond and yet fully supported by friends and family. Thoreau was fed regularly by others, and his clothes were washed weekly by his mother. Antony, like Thoreau, embarked on something new by removing himself from the nearby comforts of a community, but he was still cared for and supported by others who now travelled to him. He was, therefore, never completely alone.

Bread was brought to Antony regularly, and he remained in the deserted building for twenty years. During that time, his popularity increased, even though (Athanasius insists) Antony did not open the door to anyone, including visitors and pilgrims. The site of Antony's twenty-year home was later identified as Pispir (modern Dayr al-Maymun) and is located today 75 km (or 45 miles) south of Memphis. In the *Life,* the place is only called the "outer mountain," which indicates to readers that the place was easily accessible, unlike other monastic residences in the "inner" landscape, which could be days away from the Nile Valley.

Athanasius was a good writer who knew that his monastic audience wanted to hear about Antony. Athanasius says that the devil saw and feared Antony's popularity: "So monastic dwellings (*monastērion*) came into being in the mountains and the desert (*erēmos*) was made a city by monks" (*Life of Antony*, 14.7: trans. Vivian and Athanassakis, 93). The Greek *Life* conveys a sense of the urbanization or colonization of the Egyptian desert. However, the Coptic and Syriac versions of the *Life* differ in their rendering of the famous passage, which reflects a clearer sense of the Egyptian landscape. The Coptic *Life* reads: "[I]n this way monastic dwellings came into being in the mountains, and the desert filled with monks and they lived there, having left their homes" (*Life of Antony*, 14.7: trans. Vivian and Athanassakis, 9). The Coptic *Life* offers a less dramatic rendering in contrast to the civilizing rhetoric and narrative of the Greek *Life*. The change may reflect the difference between how residents of Alexandria, like Athanasius, may have described the events and how a monk, translating the text from Greek and living in an existing monastic community, would have described the settlement process.

As an experienced ascetic—after twenty years of relative solitude—Antony began a public phase of his monastic career as a teacher and speaker, talking about the rewards of the monastic life. As he travelled from group to group, he inspired many men to form communities and adopt asceticism. From Athanasius' account of Antony's speaking tour, we learn that other men already practised asceticism in areas throughout Egypt. The popularity of monastic living was growing, and Athanasius describes the desert mountains as filled with little monasteries as tents of holy men, all in harmony with each other and God.

The success of Antony's early efforts to inspire others and his increased popularity over his time at Pispir was not entirely good. Athanasius explains that Antony wanted to move to a place where he was less known since the constant noise of visitors was troubling. One day, he left his community of supporters, sat on the Nile's bank, and waited for a boat to take him somewhere new. While there, a voice spoke to him, saying that he needed to go to the inner desert if he wanted to get away from everything.

Antony then joined a group of desert dwellers and travelled east from the Nile with them until he reached a high mountain, later identified as Mount Colzim. Today, the site is home to the Monastery of St. Antony by the Red Sea in Wadi Arabah, roughly a six- or seven-day journey east from the Nile to the Red Sea. He was left alone at this place with some bread, Athanasius describes, and it was here that Antony finally found his home—alone and content. But, as before, Antony was not entirely alone. Desert dwellers and travellers, who regularly trekked across the Eastern Desert roads, had not only helped Antony find his new home but regularly stopped by with food for him. Soon, Antony was also visited by monks from the Nile Valley, who decided they wanted to

Figure 7. Monastery of St. Antony's by the Red Sea. Photo: Darlene L. Brooks Hedstrom.

be where Antony was. Later in his life, he was cared for by a group of companions who tended to his needs and helped record his teachings. It is unclear when a cluster of monks began to reside permanently near Antony. While others travelled to live near him, he also became more mobile, regularly returning to his first community at Pispir with his close companions. Antony also saw his sister one last time before returning to his remote, inner desert home.

One notable trip was part of an extended teaching series in which Antony debated philosophers challenging the validity of Christian belief, especially the belief that Christ was the incarnation of God. Athanasius, in his description of the debate, stresses that Antony had not been allowed to learn how to write and that, as a young child, he elected not to continue in school with his education. When Antony met with the philosophers, they were prepared to mock Antony for his lack of literacy, but Antony demonstrated his intellectual wisdom, and the philosophers were amazed at his intelligence. Athanasius uses this encounter to show Antony's natural knowledge, which comes not from formal, Classical education but from an education of the heart that comes from God.

In the conclusion of the *Life of* Antony, Athanasius portrays the monk, at age 104, as a transformative leader who fostered the popularity of the inner and outer deserts for the monastic movement. Athanasius also includes a story in which he receives Antony's sheepskin coat and tunic as a gift, further strengthening the connection between the two men (Athanasius, *Life of Antony*, 91.8–9: trans. Vivian and Athanassakis, 252–53). Athanasius concludes the *Life* by explaining that numerous men abandoned their positions, wealth, and family in order to imitate Antony; young women, meanwhile, broke off their engagements and lived lives of virginity after seeing Antony, even at a distance.[6]

In the end, the *Life of Antony* served many functions for Athanasius. First, the *Life* presented Antony as a defender of Nicene Christianity and as a model of Christian philosophy. Antony's humility and scriptural knowledge made him a legitimate warrior against the Arian heresy and a skilled orator against secular philosophy. Second, by writing the biography of the most famous monk of the day, Athanasius forged a link between the ecclesiastical authorities in urban centres and the more amorphous monastic movement. Antony, therefore, modelled the way independent monks should abide by the authority in Alexandria. Third, Athanasius helped forge the idea of Antony as an enterprising Desert Ascetic who tamed the desert by inspiring others to leave their homes and take up residency in monastic villages dedicated to holy living.

The intense popularity and dissemination of the *Life of Antony* were significant enough that later monastic authors did not need to include supplementary information about the

---

6 *Life of Antony*, 88.2: trans. Vivian and Athanassakis, 244–45. Later the account of Thecla, who broke off her engagement to follow Paul as an unmarried woman, would emerge as a more compelling model for women to follow. See Jeremy W. Barrier, *The Acts of Paul and Thecla: A Critical Introduction and Commentary* (Tübingen: Mohr Siebeck, 2009).

monk. This may explain why Palladius, writing about sixty years later, does not devote a biographical chapter on Antony in his *Lausiac History* and why fifth-century church historians Sozomen and Socrates direct readers only to read Athanasius's *Life of Antony* rather than offer any additional information. Even now, monks still turn to the *Life of Antony* as a source of inspiration, and Athanasius' biography continues to impart important lessons about how to live a pious life, how to engage with temptations, and how to understand a monk's curious place apart from but still a part of the world.

Athanasius' portrait of Antony became an immediate bestseller. Antony, in the hands of Athanasius, was so stirring that Augustine of Hippo (354–430), in North Africa, cited the *Life of Antony* as an inspiration for his conversion to Christianity (*Confessions*, bk. 8, chap. 6). The power of Athanasius's words and the endorsement of Augustine made the *Life of Antony* extremely popular. The Greek original was immediately copied, and the story was translated twice into Latin within a decade of its first release in 358. After that, the *Life* was translated into many other major languages of the Christian world: Arabic, Armenian, Coptic, Georgian, Ge`ez, Old Slavonic, and Syriac.

Antony in the *Sayings* and Other Monastic Accounts

Before the *Sayings* materialize in their various collections, Antony appears in other monastic accounts of the fourth and early fifth century. In Jerome's *On Illustrious Men* (c. 392/3), a catalogue of famous Christians and their writings, Jerome includes a reference to Antony: "the hermit of whom Athanasius, bishop of Alexandria, composed a *Life* in an excellent volume, [and who] sent seven letters of apostolic sense and preaching in Coptic to various monasteries, which have been translated into Greek, the chief one of which is addressed, *To the Monks of Arsinoe*."[7] Later, trying to challenge the success

---

7 *De viris illustribus* 88: Antony the Monk. Cited from Jerome, *On*

of the *Life of Antony*, Jerome set about to write a Latin biography about another Egyptian monk who was a precursor to Antony. *The Life of Paul of Thebes* was intended to diminish the popularity of Athanasius' work, but Jerome's account of Paul of Thebes, the man who taught Antony all he knew, was never as popular as Athanasius's account.[8]

A contemporary of Jerome's was Palladius (ca. 363–431), whose *Lausiac History* provided seventy-one miniature biographies of ascetic men and women from Egypt and the Levant. Palladius's Antony is embedded in second-hand accounts of monks who trained with the famous ascetic or knew stories about him. Palladius also references the *Life of Antony* in his account. Because Palladius lived for a while at the mountain of Nitria, he had time to learn stories from senior monks who knew Antony (Palladius, *Lausiac History*, 7.6: trans. Wortley, 20). Palladius recounts a story about the relationship between Antony and Paul the Simple, a man who joined the monastic life at age sixty (Palladius, *Lausiac History*, 22: trans. Wortley, 58–62). Antony offers various challenges to Paul, some of which may seem demeaning to modern readers. At first, Antony tries to dissuade Paul from the monastic life because Paul is considered too old; but Paul is persistent. After several months, Antony acknowledges Paul's steadfast will and ability to embrace asceticism. With Antony's support, Paul eventually became a monk known for casting out demons—ones that even Antony could not take the time to battle.

In his account of Cronius of Nitria, Palladius chronicles Antony's regular travel routine from his Red Sea home to the larger monastic community at Mount Pispir (Palladius, *Lausiac History*, 21: trans. Wortley, 52–58). Apparently, Antony was known to travel every five, ten, or twenty days from his home

---

Illustrious Men, ed. and trans. Thomas P. Halton, The Fathers of the Church 100 (Washington, DC: The Catholic University of America Press, 1999), 122.

8 Tim Vivian, "A Journey to the Interior: The *Life of Paul of Thebes*, A Myth of Journeying," *American Benedictine Review* 73, no. 1 (2022): 56–88.

to the community along the Nile, depending upon the needs of those seeking help with him. Cronius was one such monk who travelled to Mount Pispir to see Antony. After waiting a few days for Antony's arrival, Cronius served as a translator for Eulogius the Alexandrian, who was being abused by a demon inhabiting a disabled person under his care. Eulogius did not speak Egyptian but wished nevertheless for Antony's help. Cronius explains that since Antony did not know Greek, Cronius served as an interpreter for both parties (Palladius, *Lausiac History*, 21.15: trans. Wortley, 57). Thus, Palladius's story from Cronius reinforces Athanasius's narrative that Antony lacked education in Greek.

By the fifth century, in the *Sayings*, Antony appears as a wise guide for monastic living. His reputation for being a difficult teacher is long behind him, and now he is a role model for all, deeply understanding the trials a monk may face while battling the self and temptation. At the opening of the *Alphabetical Collection*, Antony is introduced to readers as a monk struggling with his thoughts. He asks God for guidance on how to re-establish his path toward salvation. After voicing his request, Antony walks outside his dwelling and observes another man seated, plaiting fibres to make a rope. The unknown man, who looks like Antony, arises and starts to pray, then sits down again and resumes his craft labour. After some time, the man prays again before returning to work. While watching the man, an angel speaks to Antony and tells him to model himself after the man; in doing so, Antony can also be saved (Antony 1: *Give Me a Word*, trans. Wortley, 31). With this first story, we learn the key elements for successfully living as a monk: working with your hands and continual prayer.

Other stories of Antony highlight his wisdom in knowing that many monks wished to pursue easy pathways to salvation. Monks needed to embrace humility (Antony 7: *Give Me a Word*, trans. Wortley, 32), remain within their cells (Antony 10: *Give Me a Word*, trans. Wortley, 33), limit gossip (Antony 11: *Give Me a Word*, trans. Wortley, 33), and engage continually in prayer (Antony 16: *Give Me a Word*, trans. Wortley, 34).

Antony repeatedly answers the typical questions all Desert Ascetics were asked: How does one please God? What must one do to be saved? How should one live a successful monastic life? In his answers, Antony points out the hubris monks might have in thinking of themselves as more holy than others. The monk who foolishly thinks he can escape ordeals, Antony teaches, will not reach heaven (Antony 5: *Give Me a Word*, trans. Wortley, 32).

In one story, Antony receives a letter from the east Roman emperor summoning him to Constantinople, the imperial capital. Antony is conflicted about the request and discusses it with his disciple Paul, who wisely says: "If you go, you will be called Antony; if you do not go, Abba Antony" (Antony 31: *Give Me a Word*, trans. Wortley, 38). The story reflects the importance of one's reputation and monastic humility, which should be more important than a reception at the imperial court. The tale of imperial correspondence is also found in the *Life of Antony* when Antony receives a letter from Constantine and his two sons, Constantius and Constans. The imperial leaders wish for Antony to write letters to them, offering his spiritual guidance. Antony refuses because he does "not know how to write letters to the emperors" (*Life of Antony*, 81.4: trans. Vivian and Athanassakis, 231). Despite this, Athanasius tells his readers that Antony's companions persuaded him of the merits of advising the imperial court on how to live a holy Christian life. Even when the most esteemed Christian political leaders wanted Antony's wisdom, Antony was a reluctant teacher. Ultimately, Antony does not treat imperial leaders any differently from the monks under his care. The only goal for Antony is to live one's life in honour of God.

Conclusion

Antony of Egypt is known as the greatest of the Desert Ascetics in fourth-century Egypt. His letters highlight that he was unaware or perhaps unconcerned with his role as a founder or innovator in the monastic movement. In the letters, Antony is more concerned with following the model of Paul as a compassionate teacher. He rebukes and instructs but does not utilize his words to elevate his position or status as a teacher. The letters demonstrate his knowledge of Greek, philosophy, and Alexandrian teachings—all facets of monastic life that seem to be erased from Athanasius's *Life of Antony* and Antony's later fifth- and sixth-century depictions in the *Sayings.*

Athanasius wanted his readers to know that "Antony was known and recognized neither through written works nor through profane wisdom nor on account of any particular skill, but only through his love of God" (*Life of Antony*, 93.3: trans. Vivian and Athanassakis, 256–59). But the legacy of Antony's disinterest in traditional education directly conflicts with the fact that Antony wrote letters and that an educated Antony does appear, in passing, in the *Life of Antony* and the *Sayings.*[9] Despite these contradictions, Athanasius's Antony became larger than life, known for impressive demonstrations of holiness and a clear vision of ascetic living that set the model for later writers such as Jerome and Palladius.

Antony was not the only one forging a new path in the Egyptian desert. But because of the popularity of the *Life of Antony* and the *Sayings*, the lives of other Desert Ascetics were overshadowed. Their stories do appear in monastic accounts but also in underutilized sources, such as documentary records from Late Antique Egypt. The next chapter examines these documentary sources in order to place the *Sayings* in a broader context of papyrological evidence. The increasing attention to and interest in non-literary sources helps historians build a more diverse portrait of Egyptian desert asceticism.

---

9 *Monastic Education in Late Antiquity: The Transformation of Classical Paideia*, ed. Lillian I. Larsen and Samuel Rubenson (Cambridge: Cambridge University Press, 2018).

Chapter 4

Monastic Literature, Letters, and Desert Ascetics

In this chapter, we move out from the shadow of Antony and the *Sayings* to explore the monastic literature of Egypt during the late fourth and fifth centuries. If it is difficult to locate the historical Antony, uncovering a full history of monks whose lives were never recorded in the *Sayings* is even harder. This does not, however, prevent us from rereading our sources with a critical eye and incorporating documentary sources, which will shed new light on the activities and lives of male and female monks.

Antony was not the only monk attracted to caves, abandoned sites, and the margins of society. Other men and women shared Antony's desire to live a new Christian life outside the social confines of marriage and family. Some of their stories appear in literature produced by other monks, such as Evagrius, John Cassian, Palladius, Jerome, and Rufinus. All these authors visited and lived at desert monastic sites in northern Egypt and wrote accounts of their experiences. Their works, along with the *Life of Antony* and the *Sayings*, create a rich body of literature with which to explore the evolution of the monastic movement.

An exciting development in the study of monasticism is the use of documentary sources from Egypt, such as letters, tax receipts, judicial accounts, and bequests written on papyri, potsherds, and stone flakes.[1] These documents contextualize stories found in monastic literature as a reflection of daily life and interactions; it is material evidence that allows us to hear conversations, follow a journey of monks with goods from one place to another, and observe the division of property between family members. Documentary evidence also brings the lives of late-antique people into sharper focus. In addition to texts written on papyrus and ceramic sherds, documentary evidence may also include epigraphic evidence such as carved inscriptions on church lintels or stone funerary markers; painted inscriptions, known as *dipinti*, on walls of monastic houses; and graffiti inscribed on the surfaces of caves, churches, alleyways, and homes.

Letters, shopping lists, graffiti, delivery receipts, and personal archives all contribute to the foundation for building a more nuanced portrait of Christian Egypt and the monastic movement. While the biographies and travelogues of Christian monastic authors were intended to teach future monks how to live, they also served as testimonies to the miracles, instructions, and biographies associated with early monasticism. The underlying biases, both intentional and unintentional, shaped their stories. As we have already observed in the previous chapter, we learn as much about Athanasius as we do Antony by reading the *Life of Antony*. It is important, therefore, to read documentary sources in conjunction *with* monastic literature to enrich our understanding of Desert Ascetics and how they were regarded by visitors and subsequent monastic communities.

Travelling to the Desert Fathers

The end of the fourth century saw several prominent monastic figures visit Egypt to spend time with Desert Ascetics. Between 372 and 380, Jerome (347–419), Rufinus of Aquileia (ca. 345–ca. 410), Palladius (ca. 363–431) and John Cassian

---

1 See the papyrological database https://papyri.info/ for more resources.

(360–435) travelled in the sites of Kellia, Nitria, and Sketis. They, and other Christian travellers, wanted to learn first-hand from the legendary desert monks. Their time of residency in the Egyptian communities greatly increased the popularity of the Desert Ascetics. After their visits, many Christians reflected on their time in Egypt by writing letters, biographies, and treatises to inspire others. Together, these works formed a body of literature with shared experiences of Egypt that were then disseminated to subsequent generations. Many of the monks in the texts are described as living extraordinary lives outside the deserts, such as in cities like the central Egyptian site of Oxyrhynchus, in nearby deserts overlooking the Nile by Lycopolis, and in cells by the Mediterranean coast and west of Alexandria.

Below, I will introduce texts written by Jerome, Rufinus, Cassian, and others to trace the ways in which monastic authors experienced Egyptian desert monasticism and presented it to their readers. These texts comprise a corpus of early monastic literature that was regarded by later generations as an accurate depiction of desert monasticism. Each text, though, was written for a particular audience and was not intended to be an anthropological field report of desert monasticism. As the brief introduction below will illustrate, this monastic literature (just as with the *Life of Antony* and the *Sayings)* needs to be read with caution, keeping in mind the author's motives for writing and the intended audience.

Jerome (347–419), a prolific author and monk from Stridon, was an educated monastic scholar who travelled throughout the eastern Mediterranean looking for enriching spiritual experiences. In 385/6 he went to Egypt for the first time to visit the monks of the desert and to study in Alexandria. From Egypt, he travelled north to Bethlehem, where he partnered with Paula, a Roman widow, who used her substantial wealth to create four monastic communities, three for women and one for men.

Although Jerome did not experience Egyptian monasticism first-hand until 385, it did not stop him from writing about desert monasticism, presumably basing his accounts on what he had heard from others. The best illustration of this writing is an often-cited introduction to Egyptian monks found in a letter Jerome wrote in 383/4 to Eustochium, Paula's fifteen-year-old daughter. In the letter, Jerome, who had not yet been to Egypt, includes a short discourse about the different types of monks whom he had encountered there. He presents two groups of monks that he upholds as role models for monastic living: the cenobites, who live in a community, and the anchorites, who live alone in the desert. He applauds the self-reliant, minimalist anchorites who are the "solitaries, so called because they have withdrawn from the society of men."[2] The cenobites are also praiseworthy because they follow virtue, live in community together, and submit themselves to the authority of senior monks. In contrast, he despises the *remnuoth*, who live without a rule and in groups of two or three.[3] Unlike the anchorites and cenobites who have order and decorum to structure their life, the *remnuoth* are inconsistent in how they live and act and are thus poor models of the ascetic ideal.

Ten years after the *Letter to Eustochium*, the first accounts by monks who lived in Egypt and studied Egyptian monasticism were published. The *Inquiry about the Monks in Egypt*, more traditionally called the *History of the Monks of Egypt*, reflects the experiences of a group of monks who toured Egypt to gain first-hand experience with Egyptian monasticism.[4] Written by an anonymous monk living at the Mount of

---

2 Letter 22, §34. Cited from *The Letters of St. Jerome*, trans. Charles Christopher Mierow (New York: Newman, 1963), 170.

3 Jerome, Letter 22, §34; trans. Mierow, 169–70. Jerome casts the *remnuoth* as the most dangerous types of monks because they live without governance, go where they want to, and are boastful. John Cassian also classifies these monks as troublesome.

4 Translation of the anonymous Greek text, hereafter *Greek History of the Monks*, appears in *The Lives of the Desert Fathers*, trans. Russell. For Rufinus's Latin translation of the Greek text, hereafter *Latin History of the Monks*, see *Inquiry about the Monks in Egypt*, trans. Cain.

Olives in 395, the anonymous Greek account details the travels of seven unnamed monks from Palestine to Egypt. The group travelled to the usual locations of the desert communities in northern Egypt, but also toured central and southern Egypt, where they encountered new monastic communities.

Rufinus, who had lived in Egypt from 373 to 381, translated the Greek *History of the Monks* into Latin about a decade later, highlighting the prophetic nature of the monks as imitators of Biblical models. Since Rufinus had lived in Egypt, he amended the text and clarified details to reflect his own experience with the Desert Ascetics.[5] In the Greek and Latin prologues to the *History of the Monks*, we learn that the book was intended to satisfy the curiosity of those living on the Mount of Olives. They wish to hear how the Egyptian monks lived—their "way of life, spiritual virtues, cultivation of piety, and the firmness of the ascetic discipline" (*Latin History of the Monks of Egypt* Prologue 2: *Inquiry about the Monks in Egypt*, trans. Cain, 59–60). The Desert Ascetics are "scattered throughout the desert and separated by cells, yet they are bound together by love. They are divided from one another by their dwellings, such that no sound or accidental meeting or any idle word disturbs the repose of their silence and the concentration of their minds in pursuit of divine things" (*Greek History of the Monks* Prologue 7: *Lives of the Desert Fathers*, trans. Russell, 50).

The theme of Egyptian monks living in isolation and focusing solely on ascetic living was reinforced by the works of John Cassian, who lived for many years in the desert, first at Kellia and then at Sketis. His *Institutes* and *Conferences* provided a rich resource of monastic thought for new communities developing in Europe. Cassian recognized that what he wrote would not always transfer from the desert in Egypt to the wooded landscape of Gaul. According to Cassian, the *Institutes* offered the "external and visible life of the monks," and the *Conferences* presented the "invisible character of

---

5 See Andrew Cain's introduction for how Rufinus adds, subtracts, and elucidates the Greek text in his Latin edition of the *Greek History of the Monks: Inquiry about the Monks in Egypt*, 12–21.

the inner man" (*Conferences* Preface 1.5: trans. Ramsey, 30). In writing the two works, he hoped new monks would be inspired by the habits of Egyptian monks and their piety. The power of the Desert Ascetics in the *Institutes* and the *Conferences* would be evident later, as the books served as the foundation for Benedict of Nursia's (ca. 480–545) rules for Western monasticism. Thus, Cassian's recrafting of Egyptian desert monasticism for the monks of Gaul helped pave the way for a complex reception history of Egyptian desert monasticism in the West.

Around the same time that Cassian wrote the *Institutes* and the *Conferences*, Palladius composed the *Lausiac History*, which he presented in 420 to Bishop Lausus in Constantinople. Composed in Greek, Palladius collected seventy "tales of the fathers (both male and female), both those that I have seen and those of whom I have heard, the ones with whom I lived, too, in the Egyptian desert, Libya, the Thebaid, Syene (where the ones called Tabennesiotes are), then in Mesopotamia, Palestine, and Syria and the regions of the West, Rome, Campania, and thereabouts" (*Lausiac History*, Prologue 3: trans. Wortley, 2). For his Egyptian residency, Palladius lived at Nitria and Kellia, where he trained with Evagrius, a revered teacher from Kellia, from 388 to 399.

Unlike the other works discussed above, the *Lausiac History* was not written for a monastic audience but rather for an elite court community of Christians in Constantinople. In it, Palladius, attuned to the curiosities of his Constantinopolitan readers, crafts biographies that include examples of monks excelling at monastic life and others failing at it. It is perhaps not surprising to learn that those who enjoyed horseracing, visiting the theatre, eating opulent meals, or living in the city were often unable to succeed as monks. But Palladius knew his audience, and he includes many more moderate portraits of desert living. Unlike his colleague Cassian, Palladius does not present severe austerity as the only path to salvation. In his description of the monks of Nitria, for example, we are told the monks follow: "various ways of life, each one according to his ability and wishes, so it is possible for them to live alone or in pairs or together in larger numbers" (*Lausiac History* 7.2: Wortley, 18). The Nitrian monks were known for their linen textile work and for making wine; both products were used to help the monks provide for themselves. The monks even had their own pastry chef, which indicates that Desert Ascetics were not living only on bread and water.

All the sources above, written prior to the collection and publication of the *Sayings*, describe elements of late-fourth-century Egyptian monasticism. Most of the Christians who read Cassian, Palladius, or Jerome did not travel to Egypt, and they relied upon the stories to experience desert asceticism. Only a few Christians with disposable wealth could afford the cost of travelling to Egypt to find out if these stories were true.

It is important to stress that while Jerome, Cassian, Palladius, and Rufinus offered very popular and successful portraits of desert monasticism, their texts were written for Greek and Latin-speaking Christians in Gaul, Constantinople, and Jerusalem. How did Egyptians, writing in Greek and Coptic, describe the monastic movement? In the next two sections, I examine monastic letters and newly discovered documentary sources from Egypt, which provide a more nuanced view of desert asceticism.

Desert Ascetics as Letter Writers

While it might be difficult to truly *know* the Desert Ascetics, given the limitations of the monastic manuals and inspirational travelogues discussed above, monastic letters written by monks to other monks during the late fourth and early fifth centuries present a more intimate look at desert asceticism. Authors such as Ammonas and Evagrius display a complexity of monastic thought that is not as evident in the aforementioned accounts of monasticism, which were intended for audiences outside of Egypt. Like the letters of Antony, the preservation of the letters attributed to Ammonas and Evagrius points to the tradition of copying letters from prominent writers in the early monastic movement. The choice to copy and protect the words and ideas of some early Desert Ascetics reveals how much subsequent communities valued the instruction found in monastic epistles.[6]

Ammonas was a student of Antony's and wrote a series of letters, first in Coptic, to Egyptian monks around 360. Like Antony's, we might classify Ammonas's letters as pastoral in character, providing spiritual guidance and instruction.[7] It is unclear which group of Egyptian monks Ammonas addressed in his letters. The recipients are his "beloved" "brothers" and his "dear children" (Letter 8 and 11: *Letters of Ammonas*, trans. Chitty, 11–12 and 17–19). Ammonas's words invoke biblical passages as methods of instruction and encouragement regarding daily living. In Letter 12, he acknowledges the struggle monks faced in maintaining quietude and remaining physically within the desert. He encourages them not to give up but to take comfort in the lives of Elijah and John the Baptist, who both "withdrew into the desert alone" (Letter 12: trans. Chitty, 19–21). Ammonas understands that the temptation to leave the desert was strong. In Letter 11, he tells the brothers that he was grieved to know some monks wished to leave but reassures them that only God can direct them to do so (trans. Chitty, 17–19). The letters, therefore, highlight the lived experiences of desert ascetic leaders in guiding fellow monks not to be afraid in their suffering.

---

6 For a comprehensive overview of the tradition, including the reception and attribution of the previously discussed Pachomius letters, see Malcolm Choat, "From Letter to Letter-Collection. Monastic Epistolography in Late-Antique Egypt," in *Collecting Early Christian Letters: From the Apostle Paul to Late Antiquity*, ed. Bronwen Neil and Pauline Allen (Cambridge: Cambridge University Press, 2015), 80–93.

7 The transmission history of the letters is complex. For the Syriac letters see *Letters of Ammonas*, trans. Chitty. Bernadette McNary-Zak, *Useful Servanthood: A Study of Spiritual Formation in the Writings of Abba Ammonas*, with the Greek corpus of Ammonas in English translation by Nada Conic, Lawrence Morey, OCSO, and Richard Upsher Smith, Jr. (Collegeville: Liturgical, 2010).

In addition to recognizing the fierce landscape of the desert, Ammonas knew that living in the desert was not an entirely solitary endeavour. In Letter 4, Ammonas warns the monks to avoid gossip and comparison between themselves. He stresses that it is better to avoid the monk who is careless in his asceticism than to be potentially influenced by the bad monk. But Ammonas also stresses the value of compassion for oneself and for a struggling fellow-monk: "When you see any such people, do them good, keep them at a distance and do not mix with them. For it is they, who do not let people grow in spiritual stature" (Letter 4: trans. Chitty, 7). Although monks left their biological families in the villages and towns, they created new families in the desert. Living with others created new challenges, and Ammonas reminds them that "trials…are beneficial to the faithful. …For Abba Antony used to say to us: 'No man will be able to enter the kingdom of God without trials," a thought that would later be codified in the *Sayings* as Antony 5 (Letter 9: trans. Chitty, 12–14).

The letters of Ammonas, like those of Antony, were deemed important enough to be copied and circulated. First composed in Coptic and Greek and possibly collected in different editions, the letters were later translated into Arabic, Ge`ez, Georgian, and Syriac. The letters differ from Antony's in terms of emphasis, but together the two collections help us see the concerns of monastic teachers and the communities they guided. Whereas Antony made references to the theological tradition of Origen and Platonic philosophy, Ammonas addresses the monks in more practical terms. Ammonas's letters reveal the complex spiritual and intellectual world of monks, who were in need of support and guidance as they forged new communities in the late fourth century.

Unlike Ammonas, who was an indigenous Egyptian, Evagrius moved to Egypt from Pontus, in West Asia. His letters and other monastic writings were highly revered by monastic communities until his reputation was tainted by a link to a theological controversy. A brief biography of Evagrius will demonstrate why non-Egyptian monks such as John Cassian and Palladius travelled to Egypt to study with him and how

Evagrius became an example for others who came from wealth but wished to live as Desert Ascetics.

Evagrius began his career as a member of the educated elite in the hustle and bustle of Constantinople. After receiving a stellar education in Greek, he was ordained an archdeacon by Gregory of Nazianzus, a preeminent Byzantine theologian and bishop. Evagrius was known for his extravagant lifestyle. He wore two different sets of clothes each day and indulged in bodily pleasures, such as drinking wine to excess and eating copious amounts of good food. Clearly, he was not on the path toward ascetic living. Quickly, Evagrius found himself in the middle of a love triangle with a married woman at the imperial court. The ensuing drama was extreme, and Evagrius was encouraged to pack his bags and find his fortunes elsewhere, in Jerusalem. When Evagrius grew ill in this new city, he became acquainted with Melania, the head of an important female monastic community there. She became a confessor of sorts for him and proposed that he put his past behind him and take on the monastic habit. After he recovered, Evagrius decided to travel to Egypt by foot to see how the monks of the desert lived. In Egypt, his first stop was at the major centre of desert monasticism at Nitria. Later, he moved permanently to Kellia, where he became a teacher. He died in 399, just as the Origenist controversy crushed the monastic communities of Nitria at the hands of Theophilus of Alexandria, who wanted to eradicate Origen from monastic sites. Despite dying at age sixty, a rather young age for a monk when compared to the other famous ascetics, Evagrius wrote several works that reveal his views on imageless prayer, techniques to avoid distraction, and ways to live the monastic life. We are fortunate to have several of Evagrius's letters, which illustrate the extent of the personal relationships between monks. His letters also document the relationships, planning, and negotiations that took place when some monks set out to visit each other in the late fourth century.

As an illustration of how the letters reveal the history of desert monasticism in the fourth century, we can look at the story of Severa, a deaconess and monk living in Jerusalem who wished to visit Egypt to study with Evagrius. She wanted to bring other monks with her, because this was a once-in-a-lifetime opportunity. Rufinus writes to Evagrius on her behalf and outlines Severa's plans. But Evagrius is not keen to have Severa visit, and responds immediately by writing to Rufinus and Melania, hoping they might dissuade her from making the journey.

In the letter to Melania, Evagrius urges her to help her community of women and her "sons," and not to seek long-distance travel to "deserted places," as the journey will erode Severa's efforts to withdraw from the world (Letter 8: *Evagrius*, trans. Casiday, 61). Religious travel, in Evagrius's view, was not worth the long-term cost to a monk's spiritual aspirations. Making the pilgrimage to Kellia, he clarifies, will only introduce Severa to thousands of people, further disrupting her already-successful work as a monk. In writing to Rufinus, Evagrius acknowledges that Severa has a noble goal, but he believes that the journey will agitate her soul, and she will lose focus on her larger spiritual goals (Letters 7 and 19: *Evagrius*, trans. Casiday, 60–62). Eventually, Evagrius also writes to Severa herself, after she was successfully dissuaded from travelling to Egypt (Letter 20: *Evagrius*, trans. Casiday, 62). He praises her love for Christ and acknowledges the value of seeking a monastic education and her earnest desire to learn from him. Evagrius recommends a book to help her achieve her spiritual goals and to further enrich her monastic education without the upheaval of long-distance travel.

The letters from Ammonas and Evagrius, as a sample of the broader epistolary tradition of early Egyptian monasticism, advance a different perspective on the monastic movement. We gain more context for how monks visited each other, the spiritual cost of visitations, and the difficulties caused by living in desert communities. While the later *Sayings* present memorable wise words and models of monastic living, the letters offer a richer layer of historical context about the lived experience of desert asceticism in the fourth century.

Documentary Letters and Accounts of Desert Ascetics

Documentary sources recovered from Egyptian sites offer further evidence of early monasticism. These sources differ from monastic literary sources, such as the letters, travelogues, and histories presented above. Documentary sources were rarely copied or translated into various languages for future generations, as was the case with the *Lausiac History*, the letters of Ammonas, and the *Life of Antony*. Private letters, economic accounts, judicial records, and wills are classified as documentary sources because they reflect interactions between individuals and institutions within a fixed moment in time. Such texts are rarely expected to be reread by many others. Documentary sources, then, are more transitory and reflect elements of daily life—they are like our police reports, deeds, wills, emails, and text messages. A few examples from the corpus of documentary evidence will illustrate how connected early monks were to the nonmonastic communities around them. These sources can provide a more accurate reflection of what monks were doing as they navigated their spiritual lives within complex networks of diverse communities.

A Greek petition from 324 CE from the village of Karanis describes the harrowing experience of Isidoros, who was in a dispute with two other farmers, Pamounis and Harpalos, and their cow.[8] One day, Isidoros discovered the cow damaging his crops and seized it. Quickly, Isidoros was confronted by the two farmers carrying a large club. They beat Isidoros and took their cow back with them. Isidoros reports in the account that he thought he would be left for dead if not for the arrival of deacon Antoninus and a monk (*monachos*) named Isaac. The monk and the deacon happened to be walking through the fields, discovered Isidoros, and saved him. After the incident, Isidoros reported the assault to the regional commandant, expecting

---

8 *P.Col.* VII.171=*P.Coll.Youtie* II.77. For an image of the text, a Greek text, and an English translation see https://papyri.info/hgv/10525.

him to punish the two farmers and require them to provide financial compensation. The petition is the earliest known attestation to the word *monachos* in Egyptian documentary sources. It raises immediate questions about what the word *monachos* meant in the early fourth century and about who Isaac was.

The monk and the deacon witnessed what happened to Isidoros, but they are not the subject of the account. We do not know, for example, where Isaac lived, what type of monasticism he practised, or why he was walking with the deacon. Some scholars have argued that Isaac cannot be a desert monk, as he was closely associated with the affairs of the city of Karanis in the Fayyum. However, we know that monks considered the outer desert to be on the boundaries of villages and towns. There is no archaeological evidence, as of yet, for monasteries at Karanis in the fourth or later centuries. Was Isaac like Antony and the other ascetics who lived on the edges of their towns? Or was he one of many monks who lived inside the town itself? While we cannot answer these questions from this short petition, we can mark the first use of *monachos* in our documentary sources and know that certain individuals like Isaac were granted a descriptor that set them apart from other Christians.

In order to trace the presence of other monks not found in monastic literature, we can look at other fourth-century private letters. In 340–350 CE, just a few years before Antony died, a woman named Valeria wrote to Apa Papnouthios (Paphnutius) about her medical distress and her hope that he could help alleviate her pain.[9] Valeria suffered from a respiratory illness and wrote to the monk with the express belief that his prayers might heal her. In another letter, Herakleides wrote to Papnouthios asking the same.[10] Herakleides also

---

9 *P.Lond.* 6.1926. For English translation and discussion see Roger Bagnall and Raffaella Cribiore, *Women's Letters from Ancient Egypt, 300 BC–AD 800* (Ann Arbor: University of Michigan Press, 2015), 205–6. For Greek text see https://papyri.info/ddbdp/p.lond;6;1926.

10 *P.Lond.* 6.1928. Bell, *Jews and Christians in Egypt*, 114–15. For Greek text see https://papyri.info/ddbdp/p.lond;6;1928.

requested holy oil, which he believed would help speed along the healing process. These requests for holy and medicinal help reflect the relationships that some Christians had with monks as healers within their local communities.

Some private letters involve monks acting as financial representatives in the fourth century. For example, Proteria, a woman living somewhere near Nag Hammadi, wrote a letter to two monks named Sansnos and Psatos in the mid-fourth century asking for their help in getting food for her donkeys.[11] The letter is not one with flowery or formulaic language. Proteria does not pay homage to their holiness, and the letter does not contain any references that might indicate whether she is a Christian or not. In fact, Proteria simply dismisses all formality; she directly asks the monks to work on her behalf by seeking out the chaff seller and sending her the costs. She concludes by offering appreciation for their help.

What is particularly noteworthy in the text is that Proteria is concise in her request. We learn nothing about her except that she has donkeys that she cares for and has the financial resources to send a boat to where the monks are to get the chaff, should they find a good price. She does not inquire whether the monks are busy with prayer or at their handcrafts nor whether the work would impinge upon their spiritual devotions. The letter suggests that Proteria, and others like her, had financial relationships with monks, which indicates that monks were more engaged with the world than the literary sources would have us believe.

A collection of fourth-century letters written to a monk named Apa Johannes (John) in Lycopolis further illustrates this point.[12] John's archive describes the life of a very busy monk engaged in the world around him. The collection includes six letters in Greek and ten in Coptic, further proof that some

---

11 *P.Nag. Hamm.* 72. For English translation and discussion see Bagnall and Cribiore, *Women's Letters*, 206–7. For Greek text see https://papyri.info/ddbdp/p.nag.hamm;;72.

12 The letters may be written to the famous John of Lycopolis, described by Palladius in the *Lausiac History*.

monks were bilingual, as were some of their correspondents. One of the letters, written in 380 CE, is from a widow name Leuchis who requests John's help in a domestic matter.[13] She specifically asks for assistance in persuading the tribune of the Goths to have his soldiers removed from her home. She expects John to act on her behalf, as he is someone who assists those in need. Leuchis believes that John will effectively motivate another male leader to assist her. She calls John pious and lord, demonstrating her lower position relative to the monk. The letter profiles how monks could participate in matters well outside the physical setting of their monastic cells and engage with women in domestic disputes.

Large collections of Christian letters were found at the site of Oxyrhynchus, located in central Egypt about 180 miles (290 km) south of Alexandria. Papyri excavated from the trash mounds of the city have provided Classicists with a treasure trove of Greek and Latin texts, along with Coptic and Arabic ones. The site is regarded as the largest collection of papyri from any site in all of Egypt. In Late Antiquity, Oxyrhynchus was known to Christian travellers as a thriving monastic centre, according to the *History of the Monks*. AnneMarie Luijendijk's work on the Christian papyri from Oxyrhynchus exposes a very different picture of the city. Instead of a city dominated by monks and monasteries, Luijendijk finds a multi-religious city with a Christian population living alongside Jews and others who practised traditional Egyptian religion. New analysis of the papyrological evidence encourages scholars to "apply an optical corrective," according to Luijendijk, to temper the hyperbolic language and portrait of Oxyrhynchus found in the *History of the Monks* and other forms of highly structured monastic literature.[14]

Further evidence of monks engaged in the financial lives of others is found in a contract from Oxyrhynchus dated to 400 CE. The document records the lease of a ground floor of a furnished house by two female monks to a Jew named Aure-

---

13 *P.Herm.* 17. For Greek text see https://papyri.info/ddbdp/p.herm;;17.

14 Luijendijk, *Greetings in the Lord*, 6.

lius Jose.[15] The two female monks are also called renouncers (*apotaktikoi*), yet they own property and lease it to others, including to someone outside of their Christian community. This document is not unique, as other texts also refer to monks called "renouncers" who nevertheless held land, owned property, and engaged in legal contracts for renting, selling and bequeathing their holdings.

In addition to owning property, monks in the fourth century were also legal guardians for family members. For instance, an adoption record from Hermopolis records a monk named Aurelius Silvanus' agreement to adopt his nephew after the death of the boy's father in 381 CE.[16] In the contract, Silvanus is identified as a renouncer, *apotaktikos*, just like the female monks who were leasing property in Oxyrhynchus. The ten-year-old boy, Paesis, is in the care of his grandmother, but with the adoption, he will now be the legal heir to the property of Silvanus, who agrees to provide food and clothing for Paesis as if the boy were his own child.

In the fifth and sixth centuries, when the *Sayings* were compiled, we have a richer corpus of documentary sources written in Greek and Coptic on papyrus, ceramic sherds, and stone. The later sources include bills of sale, wills, accounts of monasteries and churches, and numerous private letters, some of which ended up in archives in monastic communities. Some letters allow us to see fragments of how monastic books like the *Sayings* were made. A late sixth-century letter from Pesente, who lived near the *Topos* of Epiphanius in Western Thebes, instructed another monk named Peter to go to Athanasius, the craftsman, to acquire samples of goat skins since he needed good skins for his work. Other letters

---

15 *P.Oxy.* XLIV.3203. For an English translation and discussion see *Women and Society in Greek and Roman Egypt: A Sourcebook*, ed. Jane Rowlandson (Cambridge: Cambridge University Press, 1998), 79. For Greek text see https://papyri.info/ddbdp/p.oxy;44;3203.

16 *P.Lips.* I 28. For an English translation and discussion see *Women and Society*, ed. Rowlandson, 233. For Greek transcription see https://papyri.info/ddbdp/chr.mitt;;363.

Figure 8. Coptic letter written on a ceramic body shard from the monastic community in Western Thebes. New York, Metropolitan Museum of Art, *O.Epiph.* 380. Courtesy of the Metropolitan Museum of Art Open Access Initiative.

from the community speak of payments for books and the commissioning of books. While the *Sayings* were likely composed and gathered outside of Egypt, the process of gathering raw materials to make a codex and its leather cover can be found in monastic documentary sources of Egypt. It is through such sources that we learn that monks were active participants in the worlds within and outside of their monastic dwellings.

Conclusion

The literary and documentary sources discussed above tell us a great deal about Desert Ascetics serving in various roles in their communities. We observe how monks, both male and female, participated in a wide array of activities, which challenges the perception of them as living apart from the world. It is clear that monks owned things, made things, and acted as representatives within both biological and spiritual families. All these activities helped shape early monastic life in Egypt. Read collectively, the well-known literary sources and the excavated documentary sources enrich our understanding of Desert Ascetics within a broader monastic context. We can also observe how the early monastic movement was more integrated with nonmonastic communities than is evident in monastic literature. The next chapter takes us further into the archaeological material of monasticism by considering what material remains may offer that written sources cannot.

Chapter 5

Archaeology of Early Egyptian Monasticism

Egypt is a land known for its massive stone temples and tombs. Inspired by tales from the Greek historian Herodotus and the Latin historian Cassius Dio, ancient people travelled to Egypt to see the great pyramids of Giza, to enter elaborately painted tombs in Western Thebes, and to record their names on the walls of numerous Egyptian temples. More modern travellers were drawn to Egypt for the same reasons, and their names are often found carved into the same surfaces as their Greek and Roman predecessors. Egypt's antiquity was a cultural prize that other nations wished to claim, primarily through collecting artifacts and remains of mummified people and animals.

The route by which artifacts and human remains moved out of Egypt is complex. Many of Egypt's greatest artifacts are found in national museums in America, England, France, and Germany, such as the famous bust of Nefertiti, the Rosetta Stone, and the bust of Prince Ankhhaf. The decipherment of ancient Egyptian in the early nineteenth century by Jean-François Champollion fuelled the desire for ancient Egyptian antiquities. This fascination extended into popular culture when Americans and Europeans (among others) created what Scott Trafton calls the "overlapping iconographies of Orientalism and Egyptomania," in which everything from cosmetics to cigarettes to furniture was designed to look

Egyptian.[1] These products, in addition to increasing travel to Egypt, highlighted the importance of Egypt's pharaonic past. However, this fascination with Egypt did not include fascination with its Christian and Islamic past. In this chapter, I describe the fate of the archaeological remains of Egyptian monasticism amid the broader context of scholarly interest in ancient Egypt. I also explore how archaeology's evolution as a field provides fresh opportunities to rediscover the overlooked landscape of desert asceticism.

Disregarding Monastic Remains

Late antique paintings of Christian saints are still visible on columns of the colonnade of Pharaoh Thutmose III (r. 1479–1425 BCE) at Karnak. Visitors to Egypt can also find Greek and Coptic graffiti inscribed and Christian images painted on the walls of many pharaonic temples and tombs. These are all clues to the Christian and monastic reuse of older monuments. In the nineteenth century, this evidence of Christian presence was regarded as a sign of violent occupation and destruction of the pagan past by zealots. Now, however, scholars regard the material markers of religious activity as reflections of Christian and monastic participation in a long history of recognizing the sacred nature of older places. In order to understand why this idea is new, we need to look at the ways in which nineteenth- and early twentieth-century scholars assessed the presence of early Christians and, in particular, the places where monks started living and leaving behind material evidence.

When travellers and scholars arrived in Egypt in the nineteenth century, they immediately encountered Egypt's Roman, Christian, and Islamic history, all of which came well after the Pharaonic era. Egypt's landscape from Alexandria to Aswan was marked by monuments of late antique and medieval Egypt. But these sites were overshadowed by the pyra-

---

I Scott Trafton, *Egypt Land: Race and Nineteenth-Century American Egyptomania* (Durham: Duke University Press, 2004), 175.

Figure 9. Painted portrait of a Christian saint or monk, with a halo, painted over the ancient pharaonic column within the Festival Hall of Thutmose III at Karnak. Photo: Darlene L. Brooks Hedstrom.

mids in Giza, painted tombs along the Nile, and temples of breathtaking size. Egypt's Christian and Islamic history was largely too modern and too different to be considered of any real value. Like late-antique travelogues of Christian pilgrimage to Egyptian monastic communities, nineteenth-century travelogues recommended the sites that engendered the most awe and wonder. The modern authors dismissed many sites as being of lesser interest and thereby lesser value if they contained Christian and Islamic remains.

One way that ancient Egypt was characterized as a legitimate civilization with which nineteenth-century audiences could identify was by reading ancient Egyptians as ancestors of white people.[2] This racial narrative also allowed for the denigration of contemporary Egyptians, regardless of religious identity, as non-white, thereby enabling foreign scholars, collectors, and museum keepers to become caretakers of Egypt's material past.[3] In the eyes of colonizing archaeologists, it was entirely appropriate to strip away the offending remnants of the Christian and Islamic settlements to restore ancient Egypt to its "noble" foundations.

In *The Ruins Lesson: Meaning and Material in Western Culture,* Susan Stewart explains that the archaeological remains of ancient civilizations became mental pathways for Western scholars to employ in crafting their own identities, as evidenced by the displays of antiquity in museums and private collections. When the material artifacts of history, now coded as the product of white communities and not black or African communities, were disrupted or harmed, western archaeologists and scholars intervened to "save" the past.[4] The model of intervention and caretaking, especially by French and British specialists, was endorsed, and at times encouraged, by

---

2 The scholarship on the topic of race and ethnicity in Ancient Egypt is extensive. Recent works, which include reference to prior scholarship, provide an overview of the historiography regarding making Egyptians white, like the Greeks and the Romans. See Uroš Matić, *Ethnic Identities in the Land of the Pharaohs: Past and Present Approaches in Egyptology* (Cambridge: Cambridge University Press, 2020); Herbert J. Foster, "The Ethnicity of the Ancient Egyptians," *Journal of Black Studies* 5, no. 2 (1974): 175–91; Thomas Schneider, "Ethnic Identities in Ancient Egypt and the Identity of Egyptology: Towards a 'Trans-Egyptology'," *Journal of Egyptian History* 11, no. 1–2 (2018): 243–46.

3 Lindsay J. Ambridge, "Imperialism and Racial Geography in James Henry Breasted's *Ancient Times, a History of the Early World*," *Journal of Egyptian History* 5 (2012): 12–33.

4 Debbie Challis, *The Archaeology of Race: The Eugenic Ideas of Francis Galton and Flinders Petrie* (London: Bloomsbury, 2014).

Muhammad Ali (r. 1805–1848 CE) and his successors, who ruled Khedival Egypt.

In general guidebooks from the time, we can observe a language of indifference to and frustration with the presence of post-Pharaonic remains. For instance, most English-speaking travellers carried Karl Baedeker's famous *Handbook for Travellers*. They read about how ancient tombs and temples were "used by the monks as a dwelling place" and how the monuments bore "mutilation of many of the inscriptions and reliefs."[5] There was little explanation about the adaptive reuse of existing stone structures as a practical solution amid a scarcity of resources. Nor did Baedeker suggest that mud brick structures made by late antique communities were worth examining. Instead, readers learned about the important work of foreign archaeologists discovering and saving ancient Egypt's remains. Additionally, Western visitors often criticized how medieval and modern Egyptians reused ancient pharaonic monuments for housing. The act of reuse was viewed as a violation of the noble past. Western scholars reasoned that if modern Egyptians, both Christian and Muslim, were disinterested in preserving the ancient Egyptian monuments, then specialists from abroad would need to step in and assume responsibility.

In reality, the remodelling of abandoned structures was a frequent practice in Egypt. Abandoned churches and cemeteries could be repurposed for the construction of mud brick housing, such as the domestic quarters found around the walls of the White Monastery in Sohag or the medieval cemeteries in Cairo. In addition to reusing existing architecture, modern Egyptians mined ancient sites for eroded mud bricks, regarded as rich fertilizer for agricultural fields. Thus, extracting and mining long-abandoned sites was a way of honouring the past and finding an entirely new value in what foreign visitors saw only as debris and clutter.

---

5 Karl Baedeker, *Egypt and the Sudan: Handbook for Travellers* (New York: Scribner, 1908), 312.

Furthermore, few foreign travellers elected to visit the existing Egyptian monasteries, instead favouring the sites of Egypt's pharaonic past. The remains of white-plaster walls, long eroded, left little impression of a Christian landscape that was the foundation of monasticism. In general, Egyptian monasteries, for their part, had little to offer tourists pursuing Egypt's architectural wonders. When monasteries were visited, visitors and collectors were surprised by the beauty and history of what was found behind the walls. In many cases, the libraries of monasteries were then depleted of important manuscripts, which are now found in international museums and libraries.

Archaeology and Christian Communities

The early archaeological study of Christianity in Egypt focused on linking the religious identity of artifacts and buildings with specific Christian communities or individuals. For example, churches that exhibited signs of significant age were identified as churches built under the patronage of Constantine and his mother, Helena. The most famous of the early churches was the White Monastery in southern Egypt, which Flinders Petrie claimed was Constantinian in date due its size and preservation. Similarly, monastic sites were often dated and attributed to the hands of early monks or hermits based on popular monastic literary sources and not on archaeological investigations of the materials found on the ground. An additional problem was that scholars did not often look beyond large religious buildings, such as temples and churches, in their effort to gain an understanding of religious populations and the evolution of settlements they inhabited.

The existence of a church hierarchy and the production of early Christian books testifies to the popularity of Christianity in Egypt, but exactly *where* Christians worshiped and lived was harder to find out without settlement archaeology. A further complication is that written sources, both literary and documentary, reveal the presence of theological divergent Christian communities. Art historian Lee Jefferson reminds us that even when we have sites and artifacts, it is very difficult to infer specific theological views from physical materials.[6] The broader context of the limitations of archaeology in association with Christian communities highlights why finding monastic Christian communities was so difficult, and the temptation to oversimplify readings of archaeological material.

If artifacts and buildings do not necessarily mirror the people who used or lived in them, then what value is there in examining archaeological evidence? The question matters because we need to understand what archaeology *can* and *cannot do*. First, the difficulty of ascribing identity to objects or sites is a reminder that when we read written sources, especially those that are intended for specific communities (like the *Life of Antony* or the *Sayings of the Desert Fathers and Mothers*), we need to remember that authors were not concerned with describing the diverse religious landscape around them. Instead, their intent was to present a compelling story of the religious heroism and holiness of early Christians and monks. We do not learn, for example, that Egyptian temples were still open and functioning in the third and fourth centuries, with priests, or that Jewish communities were found throughout Egypt. In examining documentary sources, we observe significant religious plurality in late antique Egypt, none of which is mentioned in the laudatory biographies of monastic saints. Therefore, archaeological evidence of Jewish and traditional Egyptian religious communities provides a wider lens to the past and expands our understanding of some aspects of early Egyptian Christian communities.

Material culture is useful for building a more complex portrait of the fourth century and after, when Christianity and monasticism evolved from a localized movement into a robust component of the religious landscape of the Mediterranean world. For example, we have very little archaeological

---

6 Lee M. Jefferson, "Picturing Theology: A Primer on Early Christian Art," *Religion Compass* 4, no. 7 (2010): 410–25.

evidence of the many churches said to exist in Alexandria, the heart of Christian Egypt, in the third and fourth centuries. Today, the earliest churches are found in areas further removed from the Nile, such as at Kellis in the Dakhleh Oasis, where a mud-brick church was discovered and dated, on the basis of numismatic evidence, to the fourth century. More recently, in 2021, archaeologists excavated the remains of a church at the site of Tall Ǧanūb Qaṣr al-'Aǧūz in the Bahariya Oasis. The ceramic material helps date the church to the mid-to-late fourth century.[7] The walls of one building included dipinti, which transmit a passage from Evagrius (d. 399), further illustrating the monk's popularity soon after his death. Archaeologists posit that monks lived at this site, which, given the dating, would make the church a very early monastic site. Interestingly, Tall Ǧanūb Qaṣr al-'Aǧūz does not appear in the monastic literature from late antiquity. Thus, archaeological work is providing additional information, similar to papyrological evidence, to create a more complex history of early monasticism and Christian communities in Egypt.

Archaeology and Egyptian Monasticism

The legacy of scholarly and cultural disinterest in Christian Egypt (and by extension, Egyptian monasticism) formed many of the modern misconceptions about Egypt's late antique history.[8] Tourists and scholars alike lamented in their diaries and in published works about the "Coptic ruins," which lay scattered in and around the temples and tombs like ancient trash. But despite the efforts by archaeologists in

---

7 Julie Holdal Hansen, "Unveiling the World's Oldest Known Monastery," *MF vitenskapelig høyskole*, March 13, 2021, https://www.mf.no/forskning/mf-casr/unveiling-worlds-oldest-known-monastery.

8 Darlene L. Brooks Hedstrom, "Artifacts, Archaeology, and the Archaeologist: Late Antique Material Culture and the History of Archaeology in Egypt," in *Egypt and Empire: Religious Identities from Roman to Modern Times*, ed. Elisabeth R. O'Connell (Leuven: Peeters, 2022), 71–108.

the nineteenth and early twentieth centuries to erase monastic history, there are still significant archaeological remains that can help us examine the origin of desert monasticism, the places where monks lived, and the ways in which monks shaped the landscape of late antique Egypt. Current excavations of homes, burials, and papyri at sites such as Kellis, Oxyrhynchus, Hermopolis Magna, and others point to the construction of churches in urban centres and the presence of monks, both male and female, throughout the Nile Valley. So how is twenty-first-century archaeology and scholarship changing how we view Egyptian monasticism and, specifically, desert monasticism?

First, scholars are learning to be more skeptical of the knowledge we have inherited. The *Sayings of the Desert Fathers and Mothers*, for example, hold such importance for our imagination because the stories are about individual wisdom, ascetic labour, and miracle-working. When coupled with the travelogues of Palladius or the works of Cassian, it is difficult not to rely solely on the literary tradition, if only because it is vivid. We learn the names of monks, the demons they encountered, how they spoke to each other, and how they recited the Psalms. But we do not learn much about their daily lived experiences, how they engaged with the physical environment, and whether the demons they fought were real or imagined. The *Sayings* are not eyewitness accounts of fourth-century monastic life, but rather stories intended to enrich a holy history of the monastic movement with a spiritual genealogy often tied to important monastic educational centres.

Second, archaeological work can tell us new stories about monastic life by discovering and excavating new settlements not found in monastic literature. We can examine the designs of monastic houses, the placement of graffiti on walls, and the Coptic and Greek correspondence that took place between monks and between monks and nonmonastic communities. For example, ancient Sketis is known today as Wadi Natrun and is home to four Coptic monasteries, each with large monastic communities (known today as Dayr al-Baramus, Dayr al-Suryan, Dayr Anba Bishoy, and Dayr Abu Makar, from north to south). In the desert spaces between these famous monasteries lie numerous archaeological remains of other buildings and settlements hidden by centuries of desert sand and modern agricultural farms. Monastic literature and the continuous presence of the four large monasteries has overshadowed the ruins of the smaller communities nestled in the areas between the monasteries. One site is identified as the Monastery of John the Little and is currently under examination by the Yale Monastic Archaeology Project-North.[9] Several questions may be asked when excavating the material of the structures at this site. First, who built the site? Is there evidence that it was constructed by or for monks? Second, who lived at the site? What kind of evidence would point definitively to Christian inhabitation or monastic living? Put another way: is there anything that makes these houses specifically monastic or Christian houses? Is it possible to determine the gender of the residents? Do the materials found within the buildings reveal the socio-economic status of those living there? These questions allow us to assess the *materiality of monasticism* to enhance our understanding of how desert asceticism developed.

Third, more scholars are turning to legacy archaeology to access older excavation archives that contain clues to monastic and Christian sites that may not have received as much attention in the past and yet nevertheless provide important evidence for us today. One example is the site of Philae, home to a Ptolemaic (313 BCE–CE 31) temple complex found in southern Egypt. A complex mud-brick domestic settlement with Roman and Byzantine occupation levels grew around the Ptolemaic religious structures. In 1893, European investors proposed to build a dam at Aswan, which would harm the ancient remains on the island. A plan was eventually accepted in 1895 to remove the late-antique mud brick village, which was considered debris, from the site in order

---

9 For the work at the Monastery of John the Little see https://egyptology.yale.edu/expeditions/current-expeditions/yale-monastic-archaeology-project-north-ymap-north/monastery-john.

to expose the ground levels of the ancient Ptolemaic temple complex. The clearance of the island was led by Captain H. G. Lyons, an engineer and geologist working for the Khedive's army. Lyons, who was interested in architecture and archaeology, fully documented the mud brick settlement before its removal. Working from 1895 to 1896, Lyons drew an impressive map illustrating the late antique domestic quarters built on the island. The settlement map offers one of the best illustrations of the interconnectedness between domestic settlements and religious structures and provided an early model for the ethical treatment of later material. His work documented the spatial relationship between two Christian churches built on the island's north side, the Byzantine settlement that surrounded the churches, and the older Egyptian temples and chapels. The settlement evidence helps to contextualize the repurposed pronaos of the Temple of Isis as a church dedicated to St. Stephen in the sixth century.[10] The targeted reuse of only a section of the temple and the presence of other churches in the community complicates the often-cited narrative of monks destroying Philae's temples in order to "Christianize" the site. Rather than seeing a site where Egyptian religious spaces were expunged from the landscape, we see evidence to support a complex portrait of monastic and Christian use and adaptation. Revisiting earlier excavation projects and their archival materials, if still existing, may help to recover overlooked evidence for Christian and monastic communities.

Fourth, scholars can use landscape archaeology to enrich the examination of physical environments that contain monastic settlements. Landscape archaeology considers the local environment and the imagined landscape found in historical texts. Both elements are worthwhile for considering how ancient communities, including monastic ones, ascribed meaning to specific areas and why some sites were poten-

---

10 Jitse H.F. Dijkstra, "The Fate of the Temples in Late Antique Egypt," in *The Archaeology of Late Antique "Paganism"*, ed. Luke Lavan and Michael Mulryan (Leiden: Brill, 2011), 4221–30.

Figure 10. Plan drawn in 1896 of the settlement on the island of
Philae in southern Egypt. The late antique domestic habitation
was made primarily of mud brick and was removed to allow
for a focus upon the pharaonic occupation of the island.
Courtesy of Universitätsbibliothek Heidelberg.

tially more important for monastic habitation than others.
In the case of the Desert Ascetics, looking for places where
monks first created residences is important for building a settlement map of monastic communities. Frequently, literary
sources are vague in describing monastic sites. The literature,
instead, refers to the vast inner and outer deserts without
many visual clues as to what the landscape actually looked
like to those who lived there. These descriptors were enough
for many Christian audiences who did not live in Egypt. The
central characteristic of the monastic landscape was that it
was a battlefield in need of spiritual control through monastic
habitation; this idealized landscape was perfect for fostering
spiritual strength and austerity. The physical landscape of late
antique Egypt was rarely described or presented in any detail,
and we, therefore, lack a real sense of where monks lived or
what they built. By looking for mud brick settlements on the
edges of cultivated fields and in the nearby cliffs, we can begin
to trace the history of settlements close to villages and towns.
When comparing where monks settled, the actual landscape,
with the written accounts of where they lived, the idealized

landscape, we start to see that monks were living in much closer proximity to other communities and that the deserts-cape was very near and not as remote as the texts suggest.

Landscape archaeology also considers eco-history, trawl-ing the textual and artefactual evidence for clues about how monks inhabited the natural world, how others reached them, and how monks built and designed their settlements. For example, pilgrims who visited monastic communities started their journeys in Alexandria. After leaving the city, Christian tourists crossed a landscape made up of sand dunes, marshy wetlands, lagoons, small lakes, and floodplains. They then travelled by boat, donkey, or foot to reach monastic com-munities further south. While we may wish to know more about landmarks along their journeys, monastic authors focused more on how the monks became holy monuments themselves—the act of seeing monks was more important than seeing the constructed or physical places in which they lived.[11] If we want to locate where monks lived, one way to start is by tracing ancient roadways and looking for villages that may have associated monastic sites. Landscape archae-ology provides an essential path toward building a map of monastic Egypt. One area where Egyptian landscape archae-ology is expanding is in the Delta, where many early monas-tic communities were located. Historically, the Delta was of only minor interest to early Egyptologists because it lacked the visually stunning pyramids of the Nile Valley and the mon-umental stone temples and quarry tombs of southern Egypt. When ancient sites were found in the Delta, the remains were more fragmentary and often endangered by the high water table, making excavation more challenging. Recently, Penelope Wilson's archaeological survey work in the Delta demonstrates that both environmental and economic factors impacted the rise in settlements in the later Roman and Byz-antine periods. She considers the location of sites on higher

---

11 Georgia Frank, *The Memory of the Eyes: Pilgrims to Living Saints in Christian Late Antiquity* (Berkeley: University of California Press, 2000), 73–76.

mounds to escape flooding from the inundation and the pathways people used to move goods between sites. Her survey work has located five sites: Tell Mutubis, Tell el-Khubeiza, Tell Nashawein, Tell Singar, and Mastarua, which date to late antiquity. Some sites even have ceramic material closely associated with the fourth century, bringing us closer to the early generations of desert asceticism. The Deltan archaeological survey, as an example of landscape archaeology, has great potential to reveal new places of occupation that will reshape what we know about Egyptian settlement patterns in general and also for the evolution of desert asceticism in this region. Furthermore, because documentary evidence is not easily preserved in the damp Deltan conditions, the archaeological sites become even more essential for writing monastic history.

Conclusion

Archaeology is no longer a field focused on object-gathering for museums and wealthy collectors. The field has a highly scientific and technical side, looking at environmental changes based on core sampling and the carbon and nitrogen isotope analysis of skeletal remains. Specialists such as archaeobotanists, epigraphists, geoarchaeologists, and numismatists work together with field archaeologists, ceramicists, and bioarchaeologists to study monastic sites from diverse angles. Archaeology has also embraced a more introspective view of its own past and its past practitioners. Archaeologists now pose questions about whether objects have their own lives separate from humans and consider the ways in which environments are agents that shape human behaviour. Queer archaeology, for instance, asks scholars to question heteronormative assumptions around identity to question how monks viewed their bodies and gendered identities.[12] More

---

12 For example, see Chelsea Blackmore, "How to Queer the Past Without Sex: Queer Theory, Feminisms and the Archaeology of Identity," *Archaeologies* 7, no. 1 (2011): 75–96; Enrique Moral,

robust theoretical reading strategies also demonstrate the problem with relying solely on textual sources or narrative histories, especially when they reinforce an essentialist reading of material remains. Calls to examine material remains as *physical* texts that need to be read for their emotive qualities also illustrate archaeology's dramatic shift as a discipline. All of these elements are reshaping how we approach the study of desert monasticism in Egypt.

Like monastic literature, archaeology presents the historian with a rich array of material to examine. The idea that "mute stones speak"—and thus that archaeology is a purely unbiased reflection of the past—is not useful, nor true. Objects, ostraca, buildings, and sites all require the same level of analysis and careful interrogation that we apply to written sources, whose voices and stories we have long known. Understanding the unique challenges that one faces in reading archaeological material is important as we seek to understand what makes things particularly reflective of religious communities such as the Desert Ascetics. In the next two chapters, I illustrate what archaeology can offer by looking at where monks lived and the objects associated with daily life within the desert.

"Qu(e)erying Sex and Gender in Archaeology: A Critique of the "Third" and Other Sexual Categories," *Journal of Archaeological Method and Theory* 23, no. 3 (2016): 788–809; Lara Ghisleni, Alexis M. Jordan and Emily Fioccoprile, "'Binary Finds': Deconstructing Sex and Gender Dichotomies in Archaeological Practice," *Journal of Archaeological Method and Theory* 23, no. 3 (2016): 765–87.

Chapter 6

Archaeology of Monastic Places

Monks lived in many places, including houses, naturally form-
ing caves, abandoned buildings, and villages. At other times,
monastic communities built their monasteries entirely from the
ground up. The Egyptian landscape and available local building materials often played a large role in the design of monastic settlements. The diverse spatial configurations reflected
different expressions of monasticism in which the layouts
represented the habits and values of specific communities.

Initially, it seems that monks took advantage of abandoned or seasonal buildings on the edges of property or the
outskirts of towns.[1] Fluctuations in property management in
Late Antiquity and the inability to enforce evictions may have
contributed to available housing that monks could occupy as
they moved out of their familial homes. Other monks looked
to the cliffs of the nearby high desert, where they saw open
entrances to pharaonic tombs that could be converted into
long-term residences. Reusing abandoned tombs, caves, and
houses was not a new practice. The process continued into
the modern period and was evident most recently in Western
Thebes, where the town of Gurna was nestled in and among
the tombs of the pharaonic past.[2]

---

[1] Brooks Hedstrom, *Monastic Landscape*, 101–9.

[2] Olga Bialostocka, "Colonized by the Development Discourse:
Life and Living Heritage in the Shadow of Antiquities," *Journal of*

This chapter examines the diverse locations where desert ascetics lived and the features that help us differentiate a Christian settlement from a monastic settlement. Only a few monastic sites may be confidently dated by archaeological data to the fourth century. Therefore, the material discussed below illustrates the settlements and communities of monks living in Egypt's fifth and sixth centuries, when the stories of the Desert Ascetics were first recorded and compiled. As an illustration, the site of Kellia, famously known as the *Cells* in Latin and Greek monastic literature, is examined in detail as one of the excavated sites of desert asceticism in northern Egypt.

Where Did Monks Live?

The archaeological record indicates that monks adopted a variety of spaces to inhabit. First, monks could occupy unclaimed land or abandoned buildings. Although scholars disagree about the degree of economic change that Egypt experienced in Late Antiquity, there is evidence that the size of towns and villages changed enough that some temples were abandoned or closed, and property disputes rose in an effort to claim unoccupied spaces. Monks appear as landholders in later real estate documents where they were gifted property or portions of houses. Analysis of the decline in priesthoods at local temples also demonstrates that the rules for seizing abandoned property were ambiguous, thus providing new locations for monks to resettle in if they wished to. Such choices may have engendered greater conflict with others despite the flexibility in laying claim to abandoned houses or land.

A second major location of monastic living was in spaces on the margins of villages and towns. Natural caves, abandoned quarries, and rock-cut tombs were major features of the visual landscape that Egyptians saw daily from their fields and towns. Rock-cut features provided convenient

Cultural Heritage Management and Sustainable Development 11, no. 1 (2020): 109–20.

and economical choices for monks to reside in, and alleviated the burden of building something new or carrying out extensive remodelling. These spaces were in a liminal zone, where ownership was not technically clear, contrasted with the abandoned buildings in and around villages. The use of geostructures allowed individuals a practical and environmentally wise option for housing. The rock-cut spaces and natural caves sheltered monks from sandstorms and the sun in the spring and summer months. In the winter, the spaces provided warmth and barriers from the cold.

A third choice for monks was to construct purpose-built living structures. Just as today, mud bricks were the main building material in Egypt, and monks used them to construct both small shelters and large complexes. Brickmakers used easily accessible and affordable materials such as mud, chaff, sand, and limestone chips. These bricks were more practical than fired bricks or cut stone blocks, which were labour-intensive to make.

Desert Ascetics adopted a wide array of practices for making and reshaping spaces for monastic habitation. Monks plastered walls inside dwellings, creating new surfaces on which they could inscribe Christian names and paint intercessory prayers. Sometimes, professional painters or craftsmen were commissioned to add elaborate programmes with biblical and Christian themes to monastic residences. In other cases, monastic homes were only partially finished. The diversity of the homes and their finished state may reflect the economic class of individual monks or else personal choices about aesthetics. Most houses had niches built into walls and included cooking installations for monks to prepare their meals. Exterior spaces were furnished with mud brick walls, marking the monk's residence or property and providing a modest deterrent to animals. In many cases, monks also designed small kitchen gardens, allowing them to grow food and provide visitors with meals.

The Archaeological Evidence of Desert Monasticism at Kellia

A wide array of monastic places appear in the *Sayings*, but most stories are situated in the deserts of Nitria, Kellia, and Sketis—the great centres of Egyptian desert monasticism. Only Sketis (modern Wadi an-Natrun) continued to be occupied after the medieval period. Today the region is home to four monasteries and still serves as a centre for monastic life and Christian pilgrimage. Monks had abandoned Nitria and Kellia by the ninth century, likely moving to Sketis to join one of the larger monasteries there. The memory of where Kellia and Nitria were located was lost until scholars in the twentieth century began looking in the west Delta for the locations of the two monastic centres. The *Sayings*, which along with other monastic travelogues and histories, provided a general idea of desert sites and helped scholars triangulate relative positions for the locations of Nitria and Kellia relative to Sketis. Long before the use of LIDAR and aerial photographs, this method of textual analysis was used to map the landscape and identify Nitria, which was found in the 1930s. Dating the sites involved using ceramic, numismatic, and epigraphic evidence, which provided a relative chronology for the settlements. Although all three sites are linked to monastic founders of the fourth century, the earliest physical evidence of monasticism at the sites can only be dated to the early or mid-fifth century. A few examples below provide an illustration of the diversity of monastic settlements at Kellia, especially expressions of what we may call "desert monasticism" as opposed to "rural" or "urban monasticism" in various villages and towns.

Kellia was identified in 1964 by a team of French and Swiss archaeologists. The site spreads out over nine dense clusters of structures, totalling over fifteen hundred buildings and covering an area of 126 km^2. In many ways, Kellia was a small monastic town. Two of the nine clusters were identified as part of a subdivision of Kellia known in monastic sources as Pherme, which served as a quieter retreat from the epicentre of monastic Kellia.[3] The discovery of Kellia and Pherme produced a wealth of physical evidence, including a number of purpose-built structures made as homes for monks. The discovery forever changed our understanding of monasticism: monks lived close to each other, employed a variety of building techniques not recorded in written sources, and Kellia survived as a monastic centre centuries after the Arab conquest.

Kellia's reputation as a hub for monastic education had grown quickly; before long, Christian visitors had started to arrive from around the Mediterranean. The physical growth of the settlement mirrors the popularity of the stories associated with Desert Ascetics at Kellia. The influx of guests required the monks to expand their buildings to accommodate long-term monastic visitors and the ever-increasing number of Christian pilgrims. In addition to the hundreds of multi-roomed monastic residences, Kellia offered large halls for visitors, including new martyr shrines and a number of small churches. Because of the settlement's size, only a small percentage of the buildings have been fully excavated. The buildings were made primarily of mud bricks covered with plaster. Several residences were remodelled, expanded, and even joined to other buildings as the community's needs changed from the fifth century until the ninth. The site was never reinhabited, which helped to preserve the extensive remains for archaeological study.

Clues from Kellia's buildings, paintings, and epigraphic corpus help us better understand the archaeology of desert asceticism. Kellia is located in the Nile Delta, where the high water table makes it very difficult for biological remains to survive into the modern period. Meanwhile, the arid climate and a lower water table in central and southern Egypt help preserve materials like papyri, leather, and in-ground burials. In Kellia, therefore, very little documentary evidence has

---

3 Recent work at Pherme was completed by the Yale Monastic Archaeology Project—North (YMAP). https://egyptology.yale.edu/expeditions/current-expeditions/yale-monastic-archaeology-project-north-ymap-north/kellia-and-pherme.

survived. There is not, for example, a monastic dump pile of texts like the one found at Oxyrhynchus or private archives like those found in Western Thebes. Perhaps more surprising is that we do not even have many ostraca, which are found at so many other monastic sites in central and southern Egypt. Of the few texts that have been found, one specifically references the church at Kellia, which is our only indication that the site was known as "Kellia" by its residents.

It is not known exactly where monks from the monastic community at Kellia were buried. Without this evidence, we will never know what food monks ate, what their relative health was over time, what their life expectancies were, or what funerary practices were used to commemorate their deaths. In cases where human remains can be located at monastic sites, bioarchaeological analysis of dental enamel, isotopes, and pathological conditions of interred bodies can enrich our understanding of where monks were born, their diet, and the types of diseases they faced during life. We can also learn about monastic life expectancy, and may even sometimes learn if monks suffered from dehydration. In the Dakhla Oasis in southwest Egypt, for example, only one-fifth of the individuals interred in the cemeteries lived beyond age fifty.[4] And while we have found few monastic cemeteries, preliminary evidence of mummified monks and skeletal remains do indicate that monks lived shorter lives than the supposed eighty years found in the *Sayings*. Analysis of skeletal remains from the fifth- and sixth-century Monastery of St. Stephen in Jerusalem illustrates that monks ate a far more variegated diet than what is dictated in monastic literature.[5]

4 Michele M. Bleuze, Sandra M Wheeler, Iana J Williams, and Tosha L Dupras, "Ontogenetic Changes in Intralimb Proportions in a Romano-Christian Period Sample from the Dakhleh Oasis, Egypt," *American Journal of Human Biology* 26, no. 2 (2014): 221–28.

5 Lesley A. Gregoricka and Susan Guise Sheridan, "Ascetic or Affluent? Byzantine Diet at the Monastic Community of St. Stephen's, Jerusalem from Stable Carbon and Nitrogen Isotopes," *Journal of Anthropological Archaeology* 32, no. 1 (2013): 63–73.

Bioarchaeological evidence like this also helps illuminate the reality of monastic living and can explain why archaeologists find evidence for a wide variety of plant and animal remains at monastic sites at Kom el-Nana and Bawit in central Egypt.[6]

At Kellia, where we may be limited in terms of traditional categories of evidence (like archives or burials), there are still extensive architectural remains: of buildings, churches, workshops, and other communal spaces. Monastic houses at Kellia exemplify the type of structures built in the late fifth and early sixth centuries, and demonstrate the ways in which subsequent generations remodelled and expanded buildings to accommodate the growth in their communities.[7] It is not known who, exactly, was responsible for this new construction and later expansion. It is likely that monks, many of whom were experienced craftsmen, were responsible for supervising the design of the buildings, if not directly partaking in the labour. The regular placement of niches, benches, and kitchens within each residence reflects a particularly Kellian spatial design that is not found as often in other nonmonastic domestic sites.[8] Regardless of who physically constructed the buildings, the spatial plan, with the layout of windows, air shafts, latrines, and rooms for liturgical activities, implies participation by monks who lived in and used the spaces at Kellia.

Some of the residences at Kellia were modest: at Quṣūr al-'Izayla (QIz), houses consisted of eight to ten rooms. At Quṣūr ar-Rubā'īyāt (QR), meanwhile, monastic residences had forty to fifty rooms. Most of these structures were large, consisting of more than twenty rooms, and shared core ele-

---

6 Wendy Smith, *Archaeobotanical Investigations of Agriculture at Late Antique Kom el-Nana (Tell el-Amarna)* (London: Egypt Exploration Society, 2003); W. Van Neer et al., "Salted Fish Products from the Coptic Monastery at Bawit, Egypt: Evidence from the Bones and Texts," in *The Role of Fish in Ancient Time*, ed. Heidemarie Hüster Plogmann (Rahden: Leidorf, 2007), 147–59.

7 Brooks Hedstrom, *Monastic Landscape*, 255–63.

8 Henein and Wuttmann, *Kellia II. L'Ermitage copte QR 195. I*, 244–45.

Figure 11. Remains of one monastic residence made of mud brick at Kellia. Photo: Darlene L. Brooks Hedstrom.

ments, such as a suite of rooms, dipinti, geometric or figural wall paintings, kitchens, and eastern walls with large central niches. The structures at Kellia show that monastic dwellings were comprised of multi-roomed residences starting from the middle of the fifth century, with significant expansions made during the sixth, seventh, and eighth centuries. The walls at Kellia were made of sun-dried mud brick, which was then covered with lime plaster. Many niches were built into the walls and equipped with shelving and shutter doors to form closeted cupboards. Entrances and doorways were often marked with mud-moulded pillars, decorative capitals, and panels painted to mimic stone. The bases of the walls were frequently painted white, with red borders extending along the floor.

Some rooms were entirely devoid of decorative elements and were simply covered with a whitewash over plaster. Most houses were equipped with kitchens, which consisted of a room designed specifically to hold cooking installations and a bread oven. Small storage rooms might be used for organizing grain, equipment, or bread. Roofing could vary depending on the level of protection needed in the space and the accessibility of air and light. For example, decorated rooms were often covered with a mud brick dome, which could feature window openings adorned with circular bulls-eye glass. Other spaces were roofed with a barrel vault that rose high enough to allow for windows and sloping sills at either end of the room. In work areas, such as kitchens, a reed or rush mat was used to create a simple roof, which shaded inhabitants from the sun but also allowed smoke and heat to leave the room when preparing meals.

The earliest monastic houses at Kellia appear to contain two suites of rooms set in the northwest corner of an enclosed, open-air courtyard. The latrine for the residence was built in the opposite corner of the rooms in the southeast corner of the residence. After entering the building and crossing the courtyard, monks entered a large foyer, which granted access to a suite of rooms for the resident and his pupils. The largest set of rooms was identified by the presence of a large, square hall. This room was further differentiated from other rooms in that its walls contained numerous niches outlined with geometric motifs and bands, scenes with painted Christian motifs, and inscriptions, both painted and inscribed. In some cases, these larger halls had low mud-brick benches built at the base of the walls, providing built-in seating for the residents and their guests. Two smaller rooms, roughly half the size of the square halls, attached to the large central room; these were less decorated and contained fewer built-in niches.

The second suite of rooms, smaller in overall area, mirrored the large suite of rooms. This smaller suite was closer to the residence's entrance. Unlike the primary suite, with its decorated central hall, the main room in the secondary suite was the kitchen, located at the south end. Because they were small and used only for food preparation, kitchens were not common in earlier, non-monastic domestic constructions. Therefore, the presence of a kitchen within a late antique house may be an important clue as to whether the house was used by monks. The kitchens often included a stove made of two or more small hearths and elevated on a daub and brick structure. Beehive-shaped bread ovens were usually located in one corner of the room.

Figure 12. Detail of niche at a monastic residence at Kellia with remains of paint still visible. Photo: Peter Grossmann.

The central hall of the large suite has generated the most attention from scholars of monasticism, as the walls were frequently marked with dipinti and graffiti. These wall paintings and the accompanying epigraphic evidence are difficult to date precisely if they lack biographical data in the inscriptions. Few painters signed their work, for example, and only in rare cases did scribes add an actual date to a prayer or text. Overlapping paintings and inscriptions reveal a multi-generational engagement with marking wall surfaces in the large rooms. Untangling the chronological order of the inscribed and painted texts requires a visual excavation of wall surfaces to trace how the room changed over time. We must remember that buildings have lifespans that extend well beyond the initial occupants, and thus the central rooms became spaces that accumulated many practices and meanings over time as different monastic residents and Christian visitors interacted with the surfaces of the walls.

Figure 13. A kitchen, similar to those found at Kellia, from a monastic residence at the Monastery of John the Little in modern Wadi Natrun. A three-bay hearth, on the left, sits above a floor-level niche for holding fuel. A small oven, on the right, was built of broken ceramic sherds and mud daub.
Photo: Darlene L. Brooks Hedstrom.

In modern scholarship, the large halls with dipinti and painted programs are sometimes called "oratories," meaning a place for religious activities such as the recitation of the Psalms, daily prayer, and other liturgical practices. A large, central niche on the east wall supports this reading of the space as a place for religious devotion and holy work. This interpretation is not based solely upon the ancient evidence alone but also upon modern interpretations of highly decorated spaces and how they have functioned over time. It is important to remember that rooms could be multi-functional throughout the day and evening. For example, the large rooms also show signs of damage on the floor, suggesting that daily activities, such as weaving mats or textiles, preparing food, and sleeping, could also have taken place there. Handcrafts such as weaving baskets and braiding rope could also happen within a large room. These crafts served as meditative activities for monks when not meeting guests or preparing meals. Bone hooks, found on the upper levels of the walls of the large halls, also suggest that other craft activities were taking place in the oratories beyond singing, recitation, and prayer.

The epigraphic evidence from the residences at Kellia is extensive and includes prayers, curses, and blessings, often referencing specific individuals who may have lived at Kellia or have visited the community. The inscriptions placed on the walls of the various monastic residences may help us envision how subsequent generations regarded their legacy as monks of desert monasticism. QR195, for example, is one of at least five hundred monastic buildings at the site of Quṣūr ar-Rubāʿīyāt (QR). The structure reflects the last phase of occupation at Kellia, and was built in the first half of the seventh century, just as the *Sayings of the Desert Fathers and Mothers* were growing in popularity. Like most of the residences at Kellia, the walls at QR195 were marked with dipinti and graffiti. The inscriptional evidence at QR195 includes 155 inscriptions, with only nine written in Greek and the remainder in Coptic. Six Greek inscriptions were found in one room, which was identified as a religious space based on the content of the texts, which related to liturgical offices and possibly to the ordination of deacons. The Coptic inscriptions follow the themes found throughout Kellia: petitions for mercy, commemorations of a dead monk, and *nomina sacra*.

The inscriptions within the rooms do not mention monks who appear in the *Sayings*, nor do we find quoted passages from the famous accounts. Instead, the inscriptions focus on those living within the building, visitors who travelled to Kellia, and those who died within the community. Male names appear throughout the residences, thereby lending credence to the belief that Kellia was a male, homosocial community. The men bear popular Egyptian names for Christians in the sixth and seventh centuries, such as Amoun, Kosma, Mena, Macarius, Pshoi, Pisake, Piamoun, and Paphnouti. Other men were named after biblical figures such as Abram, Elijah, Isaac, Jacob, Joseph and John.

We can also observe how desert asceticism evolved through an examination of QIZ 19/20, a monastic residence initially built as two separate residences with two suites of rooms. Over time, the two residences were joined by connecting walls, and additional rooms were added for a total of fifty-one rooms associated with the building in its final stages. The building shows evidence of seven distinct phases of expansion and remodelling. One of these phases included the construction of a small chapel in the first quarter of the seventh century, and another included building a double hall with a large kitchen about fifty years later.

The visible inscriptions recorded throughout QIZ 19/20 are far fewer than the numerous examples of painted crosses, floral and faunal motifs, and geometric patterns on the walls of other residences. Artists used red, green, black, and yellow paint to decorate the walls with peacocks, bejewelled crosses, palm trees, ships (with passengers or sailors), a unicorn, and an unmounted horseman with his horse. The horseman wears a green tunic, which the excavators interpreted as a visual indication that the monks who lived within this building supported the Greens, a chariot racing team from Constantinople often associated with the Miaphysites. Niches were outlined with geometric and floral borders and sometimes set apart with painted panels imitating stone. In one room, built-in benches were decorated with geometric patterns to create four distinct seats.

Despite the large number of rooms and the extensive painted programmes, the number of inscriptions remains small. One commemorative Coptic dipinto lists at least seven different individuals. Excavators interpreted the names of the men to be linked to the recitation of deceased members from the community, which was a liturgical event in the church's calendar. The names of the dipinto include Pato, Amoun, Pshaio, Andreas, Stephen, Peter, and Kuri. Those living within the building or visiting the various rooms of QIZ 19/20 could therefore participate in the commemoration of perpetual prayer for these deceased brothers. The names of other male monks appear elsewhere in the building: Mena, Theodore, Apoli, Agathe, Pishoi, and a deacon named Paie. A commemorative dipinto, painted in one of the suites of rooms, records a date in the reign of the emperor Maurice (582–602), and a second dipinto records the death of two men, Thous and Pareus, in 711/712 CE. Two dated dipinti and the ceramic evidence suggest the building was used from the mid-sixth century until the early eighth century.

Although the evidence from Kellia speaks directly of male monastic life, some buildings include clues to the lives of Christian women. At QR195, women appear in inscriptions as the mothers of monks who lived within the community. The presence of the women's names, such as Nonna and Maria, in a predominantly male-coded space reflects the importance of biological and familial identity even while living in a monastic community. Their names also indicate a willingness to include both mothers and fathers in male-dominated spaces. Women's names appear, and their memory (along with their sons') could be read on a regular basis by those who visited and lived at QR195. Recent work at a women's monastic community at Atripe in southern Egypt may offer clues about how female monastics marked the spaces they shared by listing their titles and tasks, much like their male counterparts at Kellia.[9]

Conclusion

Archaeology has limitations and, like texts, requires significant caution and care in analysis. Identifying the differences between the residences of Jews, Christians, and Muslims in late antique Egypt is difficult because many of the items that make a person's religious identity visible are not embedded in the architecture of their homes. In exploring the archaeology of monastic places, we may observe how Kellia, as one example, provides numerous clues to secure the identification of the site as a monastic community. The presence of painted prayers, the spatial configuration of buildings within

9 Stephen J. Davis, "Anastasia, Thecla, and Friends: Archaeological and Epigraphic Evidence from the Shenoutean Women's Monastery at Atripe," *Le Muséon* 133, no. 3–4 (2020): 259–87.

the settlements, and the design of larger rooms with fixtures for liturgical practice and manual labour all point toward an identification of the site as a monastic community and not merely the homes of lay Christians.

The writers of the *Sayings of the Desert Fathers and Mothers* composed spiritual stories of Desert Ascetics to inspire, instruct, and reorient monks on their journeys. The goal of the authors was not to create a historical landscape of actual buildings and sites, but rather a spiritual landscape of fellow Christians linked to popular centres such as Sketis, Nitria, and Kellia. The excavations at Kellia were remarkable because they broke apart the literary landscape that scholars had held onto since the time of Athanasius. The archaeological evidence from Kellia, among other places, suggests that desert asceticism was more complex, colourful, and messy in ways that are not reflected in the somewhat austere, colourless, and building-free portrait of desert asceticism found in the *Sayings of the Desert Fathers and Mothers*.

We learn from archaeology that monasteries continued to grow in number and in size into the medieval period and that communities easily weathered the political changes that came in the seventh century with the Arab conquest of the region. Despite earlier perceptions that desert asceticism died out, monasticism in Egypt, in fact, flourished, and the archaeological record tells a story that is not at all evident in the monastic literature alone.

Chapter 7

Monastic Archaeology and Monastic Things

The archaeology of smaller, more modest objects of daily life presents opportunities to see into people's personal lives in the past. One of the challenges of working with smaller items is to find tools for ascertaining the identity of who made or owned portable objects such as combs, rings, clothing, and tools. Artifacts of daily life may reveal an owner's personal tastes or what was simply available at the time of purchase. In the case of monastic things, excavations in Egypt have provided a wide array of evidence for looking at the *realia* of late antique desert asceticism. Cooking vessels from a kitchen, woven mats from a workroom, and discarded letters from a monk's trash all provide unique evidence for exploring how monks lived in late antique Egypt. These material remains of monasticism amplify and contextualize the famous stories of monks from the hagiographical record, providing important context that might be otherwise missed.

The *Sayings* are often read as accounts primarily describing religious life and Christian theology. Aspects of daily life appear embedded within the ascetic stories but rarely draw the attention of scholars. Three stories recounting the lives of Theodore, Arsenius, and Olympius will illuminate how a material reading of the *Sayings* enlivens the history of desert monasticism in the fifth and sixth centuries.

Monks and Their Ovens

Theodore lived alone on the desert margins when he first started his ascetic life. He quickly learned that he needed support from other monks and relocated to one of the many monastic houses at Enaton, a monastic community located at the ninth milestone west of Alexandria, along the central road to Cyrene (Theodore of Enaton 1: *Give Me a Word*, trans. Wortley, 124). By living with others, Theodore believed, he was better able to reach his spiritual goals and foster a more intimate life in continual awareness of God's presence.

Theodore and other monks baked their own bread at a shared bakery within the community, a common practice also present in nonmonastic villages. The process involved bringing dough to the bakery, kneading it, and then supervising the baking of the bread. One day, Theodore went to the bakery to prepare his two loaves. While there, he met other monks who also needed to bake, one of whom needed immediate assistance. After helping the monk, Theodore proceeded to assist others with their baking throughout the day until he was finally left alone to bake his own bread. This story focuses on Theodore's charitable work, as he placed the needs of others before his own. His willingness to support other monks illustrated that, by moving to a community with other monks, Theodore understood the importance of humility in even the basic task of preparing and baking bread. The story ends without any commentary on the lesson other monks should glean from the short account.

Rarely is the story of Theodore read as a description of the history of communal bakeries or bread production. The story is short on details, as the author assumes that his audience knows the cultural setting of communal bakeries. We, however, might ask questions: What type of bakeries, for example, allowed individuals to bake their own bread? Did such facilities exist in late antique Egypt? Did the monks use bakeries often? Although bread appears as one of the main food items in the monastic diet, rarely do the *Sayings* tell us about the preparation of bread or other meals. In examining documentary sources and archaeological evidence of bakeries and ovens, we can add context to the importance of small and large bread production within monastic communities.

Initially, monastic communities modelled their cooking and baking habits upon the patterns of production the monks knew from their individual towns and villages. It was not common for homes to have separate rooms dedicated only to cooking. Food production could happen in a variety of spaces, and it was common for many houses and even an entire neighbourhood to share communal bakeries and cooking facilities for meal preparation. For example, ovens found in the Graeco-Roman city of Karanis show that courtyards were often used as spaces for baking bread. We know from Greek, Coptic, and later Arabic wills that houses and apartments often included rights to a portion of a courtyard that was divided between several families. Owners used the courtyard for a variety of purposes, such as cooking meals or housing animals. Monks and monastic communities sometimes held rights to a portion of the village bakery or mill. By the late fifth century, monastic houses were built with private kitchens, a marked innovation and change in the spatial configuration of late antique houses. At larger monasteries, such as those at the Monastery of Apa Jeremias at Saqqara and the White Monastery of Apa Shenoute in Sohag, the kitchen was located in a centralized area that included bread ovens and communal halls for eating the shared meals.

Bread ovens take slightly different forms but are easily recognized in an archaeological context. The ovens are usually beehive in shape and stand about one meter high, roughly waist height, to allow a baker to add fuel at the oven's base and to add bread to the interior walls. David D. E. Depraetere studied 113 Egyptian bread ovens from the Hellenistic to the Late Antique period to consider the various methods for preparing bread. He identified four main types of ovens and illustrated the commonality of courtyard bakeries and bread ovens over the span of nearly eight hundred years.[1] As we

---

1 David D. E. Depraetere, "A Comparative Study on the Construction and the Use of the Domestic Bread Oven in Egypt during the Graeco-

Figure 14. Ovens from the refectory kitchen at the Monastery of
Apa Jeremias at Saqqara, Egypt. J. E. Quibell,
Excavations at Saqqara, 1906-1907
(Cairo: Institut français d'archéologie orientale, 1908), plate X.

move into the Late Antique period, more ovens appear inside
home kitchens, reflecting a trend started within monastic
communities.

Some bread ovens are similar to those found in the communal kitchen at the Monastery of Apa Jeremias. The large
ovens were made of mud bricks and stone. The ovens sit at
one end of a large room, providing enough access for a baker
to work efficiently with large boards of kneaded loaves to
feed a large community. Smaller ovens, like those found at
Kellia and Sketis, would also be used for bread production,
but on a much smaller scale. These are perhaps similar to the
ovens in the bakery at Enaton where Theodore and his fellow
monks baked their little loaves.

Roman and Late Antique/Early Byzantine Period," *Mitteilungen des
Deutschen Archäologischen Instituts, Abteilung Kairo* 58 (2002): 119–56.

Sometimes the number of bakeries or mills would convey to ancient audiences the size of a town or city. For example, when Palladius described the desert ascetic community at Nitria, he presented the size of the site in terms of its seven bakeries, which he claimed could feed a community of 5600 monks (Palladius, *Lausiac History*, 7.2: trans. Wortley (2015), 18–19). While scholars may question the size of the monastic population reported by Palladius, it is important to note that part of how he classified the impressive size of the community was by discussing its bakeries, which would have held several ovens. By drawing attention to these physical ovens, we may better envision the wider context of monks baking bread and the importance of bakeries in desert asceticism.

Monks and Their Bedding

On the western border of the Delta, meanwhile, Arsenius found himself at the centre of gossip and speculation (Arsenius 36: *Give Me a Word*, trans. Wortley, 49). As a monk who was once a teacher at the imperial court in Constantinople, he gave up a career surrounded by luxury to live with Egyptian Desert Ascetics. His asceticism was of a slightly different kind than that of those around him. He was known to keep small pillows and sometimes even a mattress in his bedroom. These materials of luxury spawned complaints from grumbling monks who felt that Arsenius had a more comfortable lifestyle than they did. Where was his sacrifice? How much was he trying to tame his body's desires when he slept so comfortably?

The *Sayings* explain that while Arsenius owned such items, his austerity in the monastery was still appropriate, relative to the luxury he was once accustomed to. Because his sacrifice was sufficiently proportional, Arsenius lived a valid form of asceticism. The *Sayings* also relate that the monk who complained about Arsenius had been a local shepherd, and in the text, he is rebuked for not realizing that in becoming a monk, he had *gained* comforts in comparison with his earlier life. This story captures the comparisons that ensued when monks lived with others and emphasizes the importance of adopting a personalized asceticism tailored to individual circumstances.

Arsenius' bedding presents a direct reminder of his prestigious origins in the capital and the status he once held at the imperial palace. The story also reveals the social expectations around sleeping equipment, the design of sleeping quarters, and the pleasure that might come with owning pillows and mattresses. The small things that Arsenius retains from his prior life are insignificant to the lesson of the story—they stand in for the privilege that the famous monk had before moving to Sketis. But the story of Arsenius' sleeping equipment nevertheless raises interesting questions about how monks lived: What types of beds did they use? Did many monks own blankets, pillows, or mattresses? Where did they sleep? How did environmental factors like heat, sand, and cold affect their sleeping choices? Some of these questions may be answered by turning to the material remains of woven textiles.

Mattresses, such as the one Arsenius was rumoured to have, were portable goods that were often sent between family members on ships sailing the Nile. Some mattresses were stuffed with feathers and cotton, whereas others were stuffed with chaff or a combination of natural materials. Monks could take their lightweight mattresses up on roofs during the warm summer months or could use them out in the fields where they worked. Many mattresses could be laid on mud brick benches or *mastabas* built in and around monastic houses.

Accounts of Desert Ascetics do not often refer to mattresses but instead reference mats for sleeping and sitting. The former shepherd who complained about Arsenius, for example, may have had a mat and not a stuffed mattress. In various discussions of desert asceticism, we learn that monks produced mats and other fibre products by hand as part of their daily work. A nearly complete straw mat from the Monastery of Epiphanius in southern Egypt can show us monastic weaving techniques and the average size of sleeping spaces.

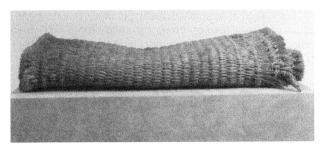

Figure 15. Woven straw mat from the Monastery of Epiphanius, Western Thebes. New York, Metropolitan Museum of Art, MET Mat sf14-1-221s1. Courtesy of the Metropolitan Museum of Art Open Access Initiative.

The mat functioned as a space for sitting during the day and could be rolled up easily and put away at any point. Mats offer an excellent example of monastic room furnishings, which are not often found in many excavated sites. Documentary letters from monastic sites reveal the personal and commercial world of handmade products like mats: monks made mats, lost track of their mats at the dwellings of others, and even sold the mats they produced to nonmonastic buyers. We also learn that monks were instructed to remain on their own mats or mattresses and not to touch the sleeping spaces of others. In this tangible way, mats and mattresses provided visual and physical boundaries between monastic bodies. We can even deduce that, in seeing Arsenius' sleeping arrangement and complaining, the former shepherd monk had entered into an intimate, private space of another monk that he should not have.

In some monasteries, we learn, monks were each provided with mats, one made of straw and one made of goat hair, along with two fleece woollen blankets. The different mats offered a range of thicknesses for comfort. Sometimes monks slept on different fibres if they wanted to create comfort or discomfort while sleeping. Fibre mats, like baskets, are not often found on display in museums because they are not considered as visually interesting or unusual as gold pendants, luxurious textiles, or vibrant icons. But in fact, if we could see more objects, such as the mat from the Monastery of Epiphanius, it may be easier to visualize the lived experience of monks in their sleeping quarters. The result of omitting such material evidence is that we miss the opportunity to incorporate the crafts and daily items made by and for monks into our history of early monasticism. The *Sayings* contain numerous stories of monks weaving mats, sitting on mats, and selling mats. It seems that *looking* at actual mats from Late Antiquity would be useful for considering the products of monastic labour.

Monks and Their Figurines

Olympius, who lived at Kellia, longed to be with a woman and struggled with his sexual desire (Olympius 2: *Give Me a Word*, trans. Wortley, 219). He decided the best way to test whether he really wanted to have sex with a woman was to create a small clay model of a woman and pretend to care for it as if she were his wife. In order to fully explore this possibility, Olympius also created a clay model of a daughter so he could also experience his skills as a father. He worked and cared for the figurines, but found the labour of tending to his little clay family exhausting. In the end, Olympius' daily obligations to the two figurines curbed his sexual desire.

The story of Olympius is an ancient tale, but it mirrors a popular assignment in modern sex education courses: students today often learn about the consequences of unprotected sex by caring for an egg or a bag of flour as though it were a child. While Olympius did not carry around a bag of flour or an uncooked egg to test his parenting skills, he did realize that he was not able to take on the extra burden and obligation of family life that could come along with sex. As with the stories of Arsenius and Theodore, the story of Olympius focuses on his awareness of what it means to live as a monk. Therefore, the story is not centred on the clay models, as they are merely tools for assisting Olympius in his spiritual growth.

Several examples of clay models of women do exist from late antique Egypt. Many are associated with traditional religious practices, and come from urban areas like Alexandria. Some are interpreted to be children's toys or mementos from Christian holy sites, purchased by women seeking apotropaic objects for personal religious practices. Small figurines of clay and bone are frequently listed in excavation and museum catalogues as "dolls." One such example is a terra-cotta female figure found at the Monastery of Apa Thomas in southern Egypt. Since the monastery was known to be exclusively for male monks, its discovery at the monastery raises interesting possibilities about its use. The figure was made of Nile silt clay and then painted with a white slip. The breasts are indicated, and the head is framed by a halo or hair. The body is pierced at the ears, the arm/wrist, and the abdomen. These piercings could have been for attaching clothing or other adornments to the figure. The punctures could also represent ailments in need of healing. Or, could the pierced areas reflect an effort to control or harm the female represented?

Small statuettes like the one from Wadi Sarga are found in great abundance at the late antique pilgrimage centre dedicated to St. Mina, in the west Delta. Over four hundred fragments of the figurine models were found during excavations at Abu Mina, many representing women nursing.

Scholars, such as Grace Stafford, consider the figurines to be important votive elements for late antique Christianity, tied specifically to the religious life of women.[2] The presence of votive statues associated with women at the male-gendered monastery of Apa Thomas may help us revise our view of monasteries and the gender we assign to objects and spaces. Some Egyptian communities cared for and raised children.[3] Could the figurines be toys belonging to children

---

2 Grace Stafford, "Early Christian Female Pilgrimage to the Shrines of Saint Menas, Saint Simeon the Elder, and Saint Thecla," *Studies in Late Antiquity* 3, no. 2 (2019): 251–93.

3 Caroline T. Schroeder, *Children and Family in Late Antique Egyptian Monasticism* (New York: Cambridge, 2021).

in the monastery? Or, could the figurine be the type of handmade, clay-pinched model that Olympius made to help him navigate his desires for sex? Could the figurine be used by female monks who also battled against *porneia*, like Syncletica? Or might the statues be used by female monks who longed to be mothers? These questions bring together the textual and artefactual evidence in a way that fosters new questions and simultaneously illuminates the lived experience of Desert Ascetics and the objects they might have owned.

Figure 16. Terracotta statuette of a female figure from the Monastery of Apa Thomas, Wadi Sarga. London, British Museum, EA73552. © Trustees of the British Museum.

Conclusion

The materiality of lived religion and daily life is a growing area of research in the study of antiquity. For much of its history, the study of monasticism was centred on the spiritual practices and theology of the Desert Ascetics, with little attention paid to where and how monks lived. While the historical and theological sources provide a critical body of evidence for examining how communities viewed their leaders, spiritual growth, and religious education, there is much to be learned from monastic archaeology. This chapter has highlighted only a few areas (bakeries, ovens, mats, and figurines) to demonstrate how materiality deepens our engagement with the early monastic movement and the world of monastic communities who produced and read the *Sayings of the Desert Fathers and Mothers*. An attention to the materiality of desert asceticism equips us with a richer portrait of religious life than what we might initially see when reading the *Sayings*.

Figure 17. A sample of the over four hundred clay figurines excavated from the pilgrimage centre of Abu Mina in northwest Egypt.
Carl Kaufmann, *Die Menasstadt und das Nationalheiligtum der
altchristlichen Aegypter in der westalexandrinischen wüste* (Leipzig:
Hiersemann, 1910), plate 73.

Conclusion

Reassembling a History of the Desert Ascetics of Egypt

Egyptian Monasticism emerged in a diverse religious land-scape that included traditional Egyptian religion, Roman religion, Judaism, and Christianity. Egypt was shaped both by this religious pluralism and the complex theological arguments that took place regarding the nature of Jesus, the interpretation of Scripture, and the correct structure of Christian education, or *paideia*. In some ways, the *Sayings* sidestep many of the contentious issues and present monks apart from the religious pluralism that existed in Alexandria and the other regions of Egypt. Desert Ascetics, the *Sayings* tell us, were focused on their individual pursuit of God and consumed by existential questions of what it meant to be a Christian living apart from one's biological family and community. But as we have seen both from the literary tradition and the archaeological evidence, monks were more engaged with their former communities than is indicated in the hagiographic Greek and Latin accounts.

This short introduction to the Desert Ascetics of Egypt is intended to illustrate new ways of thinking about desert monasticism and its history. The study of monasticism has changed dramatically in the last twenty-five years. Exciting discoveries in monastic archaeology and the continual publication of Coptic sources allow us to refine and expand the story of the monastic movement to reveal the Egyptian voices for Desert Asceticism, which is missing from the Greek and Latin sources. As expressed in the *Sayings*, the normative picture of the Desert Ascetics reflects a particular portrait of monasticism as fifth and sixth-century monastic editors crafted it. Archaeology, however, offers additional evidence of the past—in epigraphic, papyrological, architectural, artefactual, and environmental forms—to create a richer context for the lived experiences of Desert Ascetics. By integrating our new sources with more well-known ones, we can better appreciate the rich history of the monastic movement and how communities constructed a history of their origins.

First, the materiality of desert asceticism draws us into the landscape in which monks lived. We can observe the proximity of the desert settlements in relation to the Nile and the well-worn tracks travelled by people and animals. It is a myth that monks lived so far "off the grid" that they could not be found. But this is a myth only in the sense of the *physical landscape*. Monks who lived in the desert created living habits that allowed them mental and spiritual distance from the world around them, even if they were still very much physically engaged with the world: seeing pilgrims, inheriting property, selling their mats in a town, and travelling between monasteries. By looking at the landscape, then, we can better understand the ascetic disciplines of the mind and heart that shaped the deeply meditative work that monks embraced in a noisy and busy desert.

Second, the materiality of desert asceticism reveals how monks transformed the desertscape to create new towns and villages dedicated to God and holy living. Despite the call to flee the world and abandon all its trappings, documentary evidence from Egypt and the physical remains of monastic settlements tell a very different story of the monastic movement. We learn that monks worked on behalf of others as intermediaries, produced crafts in specialized workshops, sold goods that they had made, tended fields, and grew food for themselves and their communities. In many ways, monks created monastic villages that closely resembled their old communities.

Third, the materiality of desert asceticism takes us into the cells, chapels, stables, and kitchens of early monasticism. We read in monastic correspondence and wills about the things that monks owned, traded, or lost. We also hear the names of monks, both men and women, whose identities never appeared on the pages of Palladius, Jerome, or Athanasius. We can see the *things* of monastic living and better understand why visiting with a Desert Ascetic was a remarkable event. The popular tourist routes from Alexandria to the pilgrimage centre of Abu Mina and then to one of the many Egyptian monastic centres presented Christians with a well-known itinerary for Christian education and edification. The remains of woven mats, ceramic lamps, and rooms for prayer enrich our understanding of the world in which Christians and monks lived and travelled together.

As Christian celebrities, the Desert Ascetics of Egypt were powerful personalities of wisdom and inspiration. The places of desert monasticism, meanwhile, were just as important as the monks who lived there. Graffiti and dipinti marked walls of cells, apartments, and communal halls with names of monks who never appeared in the lists offered by Greek and Latin authors. To uncover the history of other Desert Ascetics, we need to read the hagiographical sources critically and ask who is missing from the stories. Knowing more about the traditional sources is essential if we wish to incorporate new evidence and establish a nuanced narrative of the Desert Ascetics.

Archaeology provides access to the stories of individuals *and* places often omitted from official histories and events of the past. For example, the site of Kellia, the great Cells of the *Sayings*, appears very differently in its physical reality than in the portrait presented in the writings of John Cassian and Evagrius, men who knew and lived the reality of Egyptian desert monasticism. Even the *Sayings*, which are later in date, present a very spartan landscape of Kellia that consists of people and the desert sand but little else that resembles the physical evidence recovered through excavation at the site.

Desert Asceticism, in many ways, runs counter to the theme of great men/great event history. Male and female monks created communities that celebrated a life that was defined by individual progress and milestones marked in the intimacy of one's dwelling. Days were structured by crafting monastic things used in daily life, not the creation of monumental works of art. Monks wrote letters to each other about payments of fish, wine, and grain, but they also used their influence to help in domestic affairs between nonmonastic parties. Monks produced books, textiles, and food for themselves and others. These activities also propelled monks to travel throughout Egypt, sometimes to villages and cities and other times to other monastic communities. The study of monastic life and desert asceticism is still, in many ways, evolving, and with the intentional integration of Egyptian evidence in all its forms, we will have a richer and more informative perspective of late antique history and archaeology.

Further Reading

Sayings of the Desert Fathers (Apophthegmata Patrum) and Mothers

The transmission hypothesis for the *Sayings* is that the *Systematic* collection uses stories found both in the *Anonymous* and the *Alphabetical* collections and therefore was compiled after the earlier collections. The *Systematic* collection was translated into Latin by the mid-sixth century. The *Systematic Sayings* eventually evolved to include the works of Isaiah of Sketis. Over the course of three hundred years, the stories ballooned from roughly seven hundred to twelve hundred.

The Anonymous Sayings of the Desert Fathers: A Select Edition and Complete English Translation. Translated by John Wortley. Cambridge: Cambridge University Press, 2013.

> This selection of the Greek *Anonymous* collection includes Greek text for the translated *Sayings*. Each entry has the notation N to refer to François Nau's work as the first scholar to assemble some of the anonymous sayings. The notations used by Wortley include Nau's numbering system for the first four hundred sayings. Wortley continues with a collection of 365 additional anonymous sayings published for the first time in English.

The Books of Elders: Sayings of the Desert Fathers: The Systematic Collection. Translated by John Wortley. Collegeville: Liturgical, 2012.

> English translation of the Greek *Systematic* collection.

Give Me a Word: The Alphabetical Sayings of the Desert Fathers. Translated by John Wortley. New York: St. Vladimir's Seminary, 2014.

English translation of the Greek *Alphabetical* collection.

Guy, Jean-Claude. *Recherches sur la tradition grecque des Apophthegmata Patrum.* Brussels: Société des Bollandistes, 1984.

Analysis of all the Greek manuscripts of the *Sayings* with a discussion of the *Anonymous* Collection.

Rubenson, Samuel. "The Formation and Reformations of the Sayings of the Desert Fathers." *Studia Patristica* 55, no. 3 (2013): 5–22.

A succinct overview of why the *Sayings* are not reflections of a fourth-century world and how the textual variations provide important and interesting information about monastic educational literature in the sixth century.

Stewart, Columba. *The World of the Desert Fathers.* Oxford: SLG, 1986.

Translation of the Greek *Anonymous* collection of Nau # 1–132.

Ward, Benedicta. *The Desert Fathers: Sayings of the Early Christian Monks.* London: Penguin, 2003.

English translation of the Latin *Systematic* collection.

——— . *The Wisdom of the Desert Fathers.* Oxford: SLG, 1986.

Translation of the Greek *Anonymous* collection of Nau # 133–396.

Additional Early Monastic Literature

Athanasius of Alexandria. *The Life of Antony: The Coptic Life and the Greek Life*. Translated by Tim Vivian and Apostolos N. Athanassakis. Kalamazoo: Cistercian, 2003.

Bell, H. Idris, ed. and trans. *Jews and Christians in Egypt*. London: British Museum, 1924.

Evagrius Ponticus. *Talking Back: A Monastic Handbook for Combating Demons*. Translated by David Brakke. Trappist, KY: Cistercian Publications, 2009.
> A collection of eight challenges a monk may face with scriptural responses and practical guides to navigate temptations.

——. *The Praktikos and Chapters on Prayer*. Translated by John Eudes Bamberger. Piscataway: Gorgias, 2009.
> Two texts on prayer and the monastic life as practised in the desert community at Kellia.

——. *Evagrius Ponticus*. Translated by A. M. Casiday. New York: Routledge, 2006.
> English translations of works by Evagrius, including four letters.

Four Desert Fathers: Pambo, Evagrius, Macarius of Egypt, and Macarius of Alexandria: Coptic Texts Relating to the Lausiac History of Palladius. Translated by John Wortley. Crestwood: St. Vladimir's Seminary, 2004.

Harmless, William. *Desert Christians: An Introduction to the Literature of Early Monasticism*. Oxford: Oxford University Press, 2004.
> Anthology of excerpts from monastic literature, primarily focused upon Egypt. Recommend reading the final chapter first, which considers the diversity of monastic experiences in Egypt.

Letters of Ammonas: Successor of Saint Antony. Translated by Derwas J. Chitty. Oxford: SLG, 1979.
> English translation of the Syriac letters of Ammonas.

The Lives of the Desert Fathers. Translated by Norman Russell. Kalamazoo: Cistercian, 1980.

> English translation of the anonymous Greek *Historia Monachorum in Aegypto*. Later translated and amended into Latin by Rufinus.

Monastica. https://monastica.ht.lu.se/.

> An open access digital collection of the *Apophthegmata Patrum* presenting manuscript traditions for Greek, Latin, Arabic, Coptic, Slavonic, and Syriac.

Palladius of Aspuna. *The Lausiac History*. Translated by John Wortley. Collegeville: Liturgical, 2015.

Rubenson, Samuel. *The Letters of Antony: Monasticism and the Making of a Saint*. Minneapolis: Fortress, 1990.

Rufinus of Aquileia. *Inquiry About the Monks in Egypt*. Translated by Andrew Cain. Washington, DC: Catholic University of America Press, 2020.

> English translation of the Latin *Historia Monachorum in Aegypto*.

Key Archaeological Sources

Blanke, Louise. *An Archaeology of Egyptian Monasticism: Settlement, Economy, and Daily Life at the White Monastery Federation*. New Haven: Yale Egyptological Series, 2019.

> Archaeological survey of the remains at the White Monastery Federation that thrived under the leadership of St. Shenoute in Sohag in southern Egypt.

Brooks Hedstrom, Darlene L. *The Monastic Landscape of Late Antique Egypt: An Archaeological Reconstruction*. Cambridge: Cambridge University Press, 2017.

> Overview of the archaeology of early Egyptian monasticism from the fifth century until the eighth century with attention to the imagined and actual landscape.

Henein, Nessim H., and Michel Wuttmann. *Kellia II. L'Ermitage copte QR 195. I. Archéologie et architecture. Plans.* Fouilles de l'IFAO 41. Cairo: Institut français d'archéologie orientale, 2000.
    Excavation report on a multi-period building, *QR 195*, that reflects Kellia's expansion from its origins until the eighth century.

Kasser, R. *Le Site monastique des Kellia (Basse-Égypte). Recherches des années 1981–1983.* Mission suisse d'archéologie copte de l'Université de Genève. Leuven: Peeters, 1984.

Studies on Egyptian Monasticism

Brooks Hedstrom, Darlene L. "Treading on Antiquity: Anglo-American Missionaries and the Religious Landscape of Nineteenth-Century Coptic Egypt." *Material Religion* 8, no. 2 (2012): 128–53.

Chin, C. M. and Caroline T. Schroeder, eds. *Melania: Early Christianity through the Life of One Family.* Oakland: University of California Press, 2017.
    Several articles examine the religious lives of Melania the Elder and Melania the Younger.

Choat, Malcolm and Maria Chiara Giorda, eds. *Writing and Communication in Early Egyptian Monasticism.* Leiden: Brill, 2017.

Evelyn-White, Hugh. *The Monasteries of Wadi'n Natrūn.* 3 vols. New York: Metropolitan Museum of Art, 1932.
    Volume 1 includes edited Coptic texts from the Monastery of Saint Macarius. Volume 2 offers a detailed history of ancient Sketis from the time of the fourth century until the medieval periods. Volume 3 includes the material remains of the four surviving monasteries in Wadi Natrun.

Foster, Herbert J. "The Ethnicity of the Ancient Egyptians." *Journal of Black Studies* 5, no. 2 (1974): 175–91.

Krawiec, Rebecca. *Shenoute and the Women of the White Monastery: Egyptian Monasticism in Late Antiquity.* Oxford: Oxford University Press, 2002.

Luijendijk, Anne Marie. *Greetings in the Lord: Early Christians and the Oxyrhynchus Papyri.* Cambridge, MA: Harvard University Press, 2008.

Mena, Peter Anthony. *Place and Identity in the Lives of Antony, Paul, and Mary of Egypt: Desert as Borderland.* London: Palgrave Macmillian, 2019.

Regnault, Lucien. *The Day-to-Day Life of the Desert Fathers in Fourth Century Egypt.* Translated by Étienne Poirer, Jr. Petersham: St. Bede's, 1999.

> English translation of Regnault's 1990 French text. Offers a wide range of topics from clothing to visitors to the presence of angelic and demonic beings.

Rousseau, Philip. *Pachomius: The Making of a Community in Fourth-Century Egypt.* Berkeley: University of California Press, 1999.

Rubenson, Samuel. "The Formation and Reformations of the Sayings of the Desert Fathers." *Studia Patristica* 55, no. 3 (2013): 5–22.

Siegal, Michal Bar-Asher. *Early Christian Monastic Literature and the Babylonian Talmud.* Cambridge: Cambridge University Press, 2013.

> Examines the genre of sayings between the Babylonian Talmudic tradition and the *Sayings of the Desert Fathers and Mothers.*

Printed and bound by CPI Group (UK) Ltd, Croydon, CR0 4YY

13/04/2025

14656453-0003